Ben. F Keith

History of Maria Creek Church

compiled from the records of the church and from the minutes of Wabash

and Union Associations

Ben. F Keith

History of Maria Creek Church
compiled from the records of the church and from the minutes of Wabash and Union Associations

ISBN/EAN: 9783337262433

Printed in Europe, USA, Canada, Australia, Japan

Cover: Foto ©Lupo / pixelio.de

More available books at **www.hansebooks.com**

HISTORY

OF

MARIA CREEK CHURCH.

CAREFULLY COMPILED FROM THE RECORDS OF THE CHURCH AND FROM THE MINUTES OF WABASH AND UNION ASSOCIATONS.

BY

BEN. F. KEITH, M. D.

AND

PUBLISHED BY AUTHORITY OF THE CHURCH.

VINCENNES, IND:
A. V CROTTS & CO., BOOK AND JOB PRINTERS.
1889.

TO MY
BELOVED BRETHREN AND SISTERS
OF
MARIA CREEK CHURCH
THE FOLLOWING HISTORY IS RESPECTFULLY
INSCRIBED.

INTRODUCTION.

MARIA CREEK CHURCH is one of the oldest Baptist churches in the State of Indiana; and is now, so far as the writer can learn, the oldest Baptist church that has had a continued existence since her organization

It had long been thought by some of her members, that her history ought to be written and put in such form as that it would be preserved; and at their request the following short history has been compiled. It is imperfect, but gives the material facts of her history as found in her records.

HISTORY
OF
MARIA CREEK CHURCH.

---o---

CHAPTER I.

In the beginning of the present century pioneers began to push out from the Eastern States into Indiana Territory.

A number of these bold, energetic men settled in what is now the northern part of Knox county, Indiana, between the Wabash and White rivers, and some of them on the west side of the Wabash river in Illinois Territory.

This country was then on the extreme western frontier, and almost an unbroken forest, full of wild animals and savage Indians, where the few settlers had continually to guard their stock from the one, and their wives and children from the other.

Most of them had come from Kentucky and Ohio, and had settled in this wild country. With strong arms they attacked the forest for the purpose of making homes for themselves and children, and with brave hearts purposed to defend them. Among these hardy pioneers were a number of Baptist people, who, with the assistance of Elder Alexander Diven, from Columbia, a little village on Patoka river in what is now Gibson, then Knox county, Indiana, and Elder James McQuaid from Kentucky, organized Maria Creek Church on the 20th day of May, 1809.

There were thirteen members that entered into that organization, viz: Samuel Allison, Phoebe Allison, Charles Polke, Sen., Charles Polke, Jr., Margaret Polke, Achsah Polke, William Polke, Sally Polke, John Lemen, Polly Lemen, William Bruce, Sally Bruce, and John Morris, a man of color.

Of the above named persons Samuel Allison, Phoebe Allison and John Morris lived on the west side of the Wabash river in Illinois Territory.

As a bond of Christian fellowship they united together and agreed on the following

ARTICLES OF FAITH:

ART. 1st. We believe in one only true and living God, eternal and immutable, the Creator and Upholder of all intelligent beings, who governs all things with righteousness according to the counsel of His own will; and that He has revealed Himself to the children of men in the Scriptures of Truth contained in the old and new Testaments, which are of Divine authority and the only infallible rule of Faith and Practice, under the three personal characters of Father, Son, and Holy Ghost.

ART. 2d. We believe that God created man upright, but by reason of his transgressions he became dead in trespasses and sins and unable to deliver himself from that state of death and misery he has fallen into.

Art. 3d. We believe that Christ Jesus was set up from everlasting as the Savior of His Church, and that in consequence of His union thereto as the Head, His righteous life, death, ressurrection and ascension, are the means by which His Church is reconciled to God.

Art. 4th. We believe that God's elect were chosen in Christ Jesus before the foundation of the world, according to His purpose and Grace; and that in time they will be effectually called by Grace, justified in the sight of God by the imputed righteousness of Jesus Christ, sanctified through the divine influence of the Holy Spirit, and shall finally persevere in Grace to Glory, and cannot finally fall away.

Art. 5th. We believe that good works are the fruits of the Faith of God's elect, and follow after they are born of the Spirit of God, and only justifies them in the sight of angels and men, and are evidences of their gracious state.

Art. 6th. We believe in the resurrection of the body, both of the just and unjust, but every one in his own order; they that have done good unto the resurrection of life, and they that have done evil unto the resurrection of damnation; and that God hath appointed a day wherein He will judge the world in righteousness by Jesus Christ.

Art. 7th. We believe the joys of the righteous will be eternal, and the punishment of the wicked of everlasting duration.

Art. 8th. We believe that Baptism by immersion on a profession of our faith, and the Lord's Supper are ordinances of God's appointment in his Church

Art. 9th. We believe that God hath set apart one day in seven for religious worship, and that the first day of the week we ought to observe as such, in resting from our temporal concerns, excepting works of necessity and mercy.

Art. 10th. We believe that African slavery as it exists in some parts of the United States, is unjust in its origin and oppressive in its consequences; and is inconsistent with the spirit of the Gospel. But viewing our situation in this Territory, as the Law does not tolerate hereditary slavery, we think it inexpedient to meddle with the subject in a Church capacity. [*See note below].

CHURCH COVENANT.

After being banded together on the foregoing doctrines, we believe it to be our duty to watch over and for each other, to conduct ourselves as becomes the followers of the meek and lowly Jesus; to keep gospel discipline in the Church, not forsaking the assembling ourselves together, but fill our places on our appointed days of meeting for business and preaching; and do such other things as God

---

*Note—It is thought by some that this 10th Article of the Confession of Faith was not adopted as an Article of Faith at the organization of the Church, but was drafted by Wm. Polke and passed as a resolution by the Church in 1815, and appended to their Articles of Faith. The records are full and perfect of every meeting through all the early years of the existence. If such action had been taken subsequent to the organization of the Church, it would have appeared in their minutes. It is therefore presumed that it was adopted at the organization of the Church, and was the first public act, so far as known by the writer, condemning slavery, by any body corporate or otherwise, in Indiana Teritory.

in His word has directed us to do. The foregoing covenant we, in the fear of God, enter into, and have subscribed our names hereunto this 20th day of May, 1809.

Being thus constituted they proceed to business by choosing William Polke Church Clerk.

Thus was planted, on the then Western frontier, Maria Creek Church. A Church that was destined to have a wide influence; not only in all that part of the country in which she was located, but on many other and far distant places, by the removal, from time to time, of persons who had been received into Her fellowship, and instructed under Her teaching in the truths of the Religion of Christ, and who carried with them the religious teaching, and Christian character thus received in Maria Creek Church.

She has thus, and by her long continuance and active Christian work at home, wielded an influence for good, and for the salvation of sinners, the extent of which will never be known until that day when the Master shall say, "well done good and faithful servants, enter thou into the joys of thy Lord."

At the third meeting of the Church they adopted the following

RULES OF DECORUM:

Rule 1st. The meeting shall be opened and closed by prayer.

Rule 2d. An invitation to members of sister churches present to take seats and give their counsel, shall be given.

Rule 3d. An enquiry to be made whether there is any matter of grievance that Gospel steps have been taken with, that is ready to come before the Church since last meeting.

Rule 4th.   Door opened for the reception of members.

Rule 5th.   References to be taken up and acted upon.

Rule 6th.   Any member may make a motion, and every motion made and seconded shall be attended to, unless withdrawn by the member who made it.

Rule 7th.   But one person to speake at a time, who shall rise from his seat and address the moderator, and while speaking shall attend strictly to the subject in hand, and shall in no wise cast any personal reflections on any person who may have spoken before him.

Rule 8th.   No person shall be interrupted in his speech by any one except the moderator, who shall call him to order if he depart from the subject in hand.

Rule 9th.   No person shall speak more than three times on the same subject without the approbation of the Church.

Rule 10th.   Each member shall keep his seat in silence while the Church is transacting her business, and shall not withdraw without the consent of the Church.

Rule 11th.   All business to be decided by a majority, except the receiving and dismissing members, and setting forward preachers, which shall be done by a unanimous vote.

Rule 12th.   The Church when organized for business shall have a Moderator and Clerk. The duty of the Moderator shall be to keep the Church in order, state all propositions fairly to the Church and take their voice thereon, shall have no vote unless the Church is equally divided, in which case he shall have the casting vote. The duty of the Clerk shall be to keep a fair record of all the proceedings of the Church.

Rule 13th. The Moderator shall have the same liberty of speech as other members, provided his seat be filled.

Rule 14th. All business to be done in public, except such as the Church shall deem of a private nature.

Rule 15th. Any member may call for order.

RESOLUTIONS.

Resolved, That we in future strive together to live up to those duties as Church and Pastor for a Gospel discippline as set forth in our rules.

Resolved, That this Church will not extend fellowship to any person who is in the habit of visiting saloons or using intoxicating drinks as a beverage.

Resolved, That delinquent members be visited and requested to attend Church; those failing to attend for three months without being providentially hindered are to be cited to attend.

Resolved, That any member who is financially able, and voluntarily refuses to contribute to the support of the Gospel, shall be disciplined.

Resolved, That we will abstain from the use of tobacco while in the house of the Lord.

Resolved, That it is the duty of any member of this Church, knowing another to be guilty of wrong, to immediately take proper Gospel steps in the matter; and failing so to do, renders such member or members liable to the discipline of the Church.

Resolved, That the action of the Church heretofore in receiving excluded members of sister Churches, shall not be made a precedent governing the future action of the Church in like cases.

WHEREAS, Balls and dancing parties are evil in their nature, and irreligious in their tendency, therefore be it

Resolved, That we abstain from such parties, and in all suitable ways discountenance such habits in this community.

These resolutions were not all adopted at the beginning of the Church, but have been passed at various times as occasion seemed to demand.

At this third meeting of the Church they invited Isaac McCoy, then a member of Silver Creek Church, Clark Co., Indiana Territory, and holding a license to preach from that Church, to visit and preach for them. Sometime in the latter part of the year 1809, he removed to Maria Creek and became the pastor of Maria Creek Church, and in January, 1810, united by letter with the Church.

On the 16th of June following the Church took into consideration the propriety of ordaining Brother Isaac McCoy to the work of the ministry. After holding the matter under consideration for two months they decided to have him ordained. They then wrote to Kentucky for ministers to come and assist in his ordination. In October following Elders George Waller and William McCoy (father of Isaac McCoy), from Buck Creek Church, Shelby Co., Ky., being present in answer to the request of the church. "After a sermon preached by Bro. Waller, suitable to the occasion, proceeded to the ordination of Bro. Isaac McCoy as a preacher, to the general satisfaction of the church."

At the first meeting of the church after they were organized, messengers or delegates were appointed to meet with like delegates from other churches, for the purpose of forming a union of churches, or an association. Delegates from five churches, to-wit: Wabash, Bethel, Salem, Patoka, and Maria Creek, met at a little village called Columbia, on Patoka river, then in Knox, now in Gibson Co., on the second Friday in July, 1809, and organized the Wabash District Association, the first association organized in this part of Indiana Territory.

From the organization of the church until the meeting in October 1810 the church had received eleven members by letter. At this meeting, the same at which Isaac McCoy was ordained, the church received her first convert, viz: Elizabeth Chambers, wife of Joseph Chambers. She, however, was not baptized at that time. Joseph Chambers says in a short sketch of his life from which I quote, "She refused to submit to the sacred ordinance from a sense of her unworthiness, until January following, when we were both baptized on the same day." But he says further, that on the day she was received a candidate for baptism he, himself, became very much concerned about his soul's salvation, and the hope that he would soon go with her was probably one reason why she waited. In the mean time, while she was waiting, Joseph Listen and his wife were received and baptized, being the first persons baptized into Maria Creek Church.

During the years of 1812 and '13 the people on the frontier were exposed to the dangers and alarms of Indian warfare. They lived in small forts and block houses scattered over the country, and at all times went armed whenever they went out of their forts, whether they went into their fields to work, or to their places of meeting to worship, prepared to fight any Indians who might be prowling around, watching for an opportunity to kill and scalp, or capture any one or more they might find unprotected. Subject to all these hardships of pioneer life, and the difficulties of obtaining the necessary food and clothing for themselves and families, yet notwithstanding all these trials and hardships, they maintained the organization of their church, and, with one or two exceptions, kept up their regular meetings. Isaac McCoy, their pastor, trusting in God and armed with his Bible and musket, traveled from fort to fort, preaching to the people, encouraging the brethren and sisters, warning sinners and inviting them to come to Christ. And thus they passed through the war, maintained the organization and prospered as a church. Not one of them was lost or hurt during the war, except their Church Clerk, William Polke, who received a wound at the Battle of Tippecanoe, from which he soon recovered.

All persons who have faith in God will readily believe that He watched over them and kept them through all these trials and dangers.

---o---

CHAPTER II.

The following extracts are copied from the church records during the earlier years of her history, for the purpose of showing something of her inside workings as a church, and of exhibiting some of the characteristics of her members, their frankness, their straight-forward honesty and singleness of purpose, and for the further purpose of illustrating, as they sometimes do, Baptist principles and doctrines. They are copied as they appear on the church records. There is, in some of them, some peculiar forms of expression, and a certain degree of quaintness, that will be of interest to those at least for whom this history is written.

"Sept., 1809. Query. What methods shall the church pursue in the reception of members who bring letters with them from churches not certifying the doctrines held by said churches. Answer. Any member to have liberty to ask questions for satisfaction."

"June 16th, 1810. Sister Elizabeth Brown handed in her letter, which not giving general satisfaction as to the doctrines held by the church from which she comes. After examination she was cordially received."

"June, 1811. Zacharia Bawls came forward with his letter, which not giving satisfaction; on examination the church conceives it prudent not to receive him; as fellowship is not obtained."

"June, 1810. Brother Kennedy handed in his license as a preacher. The church not being acquainted with Bro. Kennedy as a preacher, agrees to hear him before they give him a certificate of approbation on his license, and return the same to him."

"July, 1810. The church agrees to give Brother Kennedy a certificate of approbation on the back of his license, which he handed in last meeting and return the same to him."

"Jan., 1811. Bro. McCoy brought forward a piece he had written in answer to a pamphlet wrote by Mr. Timothy Merrit on absolute perseverence. The church after hearing said piece, gave Bro. McCoy liberty to make what use of said piece he thinks proper. March 1811. The church, after re-hearing Bro. McCoy's answer to Mr. Merrit on the perseverence of the saints, advise him to publish the same."

Would it not be well for writers of to-day on Theological subjects to submit their "pieces" to the church before publishing?

After having previously agreed to build a meeting house, and selected a place to build, the following record appears in the minutes of March, 1811:

"The church agrees to appoint Saturday, the 23d instant,

to meet for the purpose of building a meeting house, and and that we request our neighbors to assist us on that day."

It is presumed they met accordingly and built a meeting house.

"August, 1811. Bro. McCoy proceeded to read to the church a number of spiritual songs he had composed on different religious subjects, and requested the advice of the church, in what way he should act in regard to said composures. The church unanimously approve of said composures, both in respect of poetry and doctrine, and bid him God speed in the same. The church unanimously advise Bro. McCoy to make the same public in the manner that seems to him right."

"Feb., 1812. Peter Hansbrough presented a letter asking admission into the church. Objected to on account of his holding slaves, by Brethren Wm. Bruce and Wm. Drake, and by Sisters Delila Listen, Elizabeth More and Polly Chambers. Refered."

"March, 1812. The reference respecting the reception of Bro. Peter Hansbrough being taken up, the objectors being called on to know whether they continued their objections. A preparatory motion to come at the business, moved and seconded, that an enquiry be made of the church whether they wish to continue the union with the Baptists they stand united with. The church say with the exception of one member, Wm. Bruce, they wish to continue the union. The objectors to the reception of

Bro. Hansbrough being again called on, whether they still continue their objections to his reception on account of his holding slaves.

"Bro. Wm. Bruce continueing his objections and the church conceiving the objections to amount to a declaration of non-fellowship with the Baptist connexion with whom we are in union; and the church believing it will be to the advancement of the Redeemer's kingdom and the peace and prosperity of the church to continue the union, and Bro. Bruce being unwilling to continue in union with slave holders, he is considered no more a member with us: at the same time they declare they have no objections to his moral character as a christian."

Bro. Wm. Bruce was afterwards, (July, 1816,) at his request, restored to the church.

"May, 1812. Owing to our situation on the frontier, in respect to the Indian alarms, people being in a defensless situation, the church failed to meet at our april meeting; but have the satisfaction to meet together (owing to the goodness of our God) at our meeting in course on the 16th of may and in order proceeded to business.

"Received by relation Polly Thomas, who was formerly a member of the denomination called Christians or Newlights, but professing to believe the doctrines this church was constituted on, and having been Baptized by immersion, she was unanimously received a member with us."

This was the first example of alien baptism in Maria Creek Church.

"Aug., 1813. Moved, that as a number of our Brethren have failed to attend for the last three meetings, the church agrees to request them to attend in October."

A number of members were appointed to notify them to attend and give reasons for their failure. Then follows this:

"The Sisters, owing to our exposed situation on the frontier, the church thinks not proper to request their attendance."

Just think of it. Three of these absent members, living on the west side of the Wabash, fifteen miles away, were cited to attend and give reasons for their failure to attend for three meetings, and at the same time the Sisters advised not to attend on account of danger from the Indians, it being unsafe for them to leave their fort.

The record says these Brethren attended and gave satisfactory reasons for their failure. In view of all the circumstances it would be interesting to know what those reasons were.

"Jan., 1814. Polly Thomas informed the church that she had been guilty of a wrong in joining the young people on last newyears evening in their plays and pastimes, which was unbecoming a professor of religion. The church are of opinion our sister be reproved and keep her seat as a member in full fellowship, Bro. McCoy to reprove our sister, which he did in presence of the church."

"June, 1814. The church being informed that John Hansbrough, being a member of a church in Kentucky, and it being known to the church that he makes use of profane language, and other conduct unbecoming a professor of religion, the church conceives it her duty to write to Flat Rock Church, Jefferson Co., Ky., informing them of his conduct. Bro. Wm. Polke to prepare a letter and present to the church tomorrow morning. Sunday morning. The church approved the letter prepared to be sent to Flat-rock."

They watched over the brethren, whether they were members of their own church or of some other Baptist church.

Subsequently the following record appears:

"John Hansbrough, formerly a member of Flat Rock Church, who was excluded in consequence of information from this church, came forward and related that he hoped the Lord had healed his backsliding, and had loved him with an everlasting love, and with loving kindness had drawn him, which gave unanimous satisfaction and joy. On motion, the clerk directed to inform Flat Rock Church of the happy return of our Brother.

"March, 1814. The church is of opinion that any stranger travelling under the character of a Baptist preacher, be not invited to preach unless he brings a certificate from the church where he has his membership, certifying his character, or gives some other satisfaction of his standing in society."

It would be well for all churches to follow this example of Maria Creek Church.

"March, 1819. Bro. Richard Brock informed the church that he had imprudently been guilty of a wrong in correcting his daughter agreeably to a former promise he had made that if she joined the Methodists he would whip her. He expressed his sorrow that he was so unpleasantly situated as either to break his promise, or to proceed to rash measures. The church, after hearing the Brother's acknowledgement and conversing thereon, admonish the Bro. to let his moderation be known to all men, and do nothing rashly. And while we thus counsel our Bro. we wish to take the counsel to ourselves, and wish it distinctly understood that this church disapproves of all rash measures to restrain the liberty of conscience in our Families, and to use no other methods than reason and arguments drawn from the scriptures, to restrain our Families from joining any other denomination of professed Christians."

They were true to Baptist principles.

"Feb. 16th, 1811. The church agrees to raise six dollars for the use of the church one year."

"March, 1813. It appearing from the minutes of our last association that Bro. John Lemen, who was appointed by the preceding association to prepare a circular letter, has failed to prepare the same, and the association advising this church to enquire of our Brother Lemen the cause of his failure.

"Brother Lemen, being called on, stated that, owing to his situation on the frontiers, his mind was not sufficiently calm and unmoved to compose said letter; and secondly, he did not believe it his duty to attend the association, owing to the exposed situation in which he lived, and therefore thought it improper for him to write said letter as coming from the association, he not being present at the meeting thereof.

"The church unanimously are of opinion said reasons are proper."

"June, 1815. A request from the church at Lamotte for a committee to look into their standing as a church to determine whether they are in order to join the association. The church are of opinion that it would be improper to send such a committee, as it would be assuming more authority than one church ought to exercise over another."

"Oct. 1817. Brother McCoy informed the church that he had accepted an appointment from the Baptist Board of Foreign Missions for the United States, for the ensuing year; and requests of the church her approval or disapproval of his conduct. After conversation had thereon the church unanimously approve of the same."

"May, 1819. Moved that Bros. Joseph Chambers and William Keith wait on Mr. Duty and wife and inform them this church fellowship their daughter Sally as a Christian; and request their approbation to her being baptised and becoming a member with us."

They appear in this more anxious to do right than to increase their membership.

These extracts are interesting as events occurring in

the early history of the church; but they are more interesting as exhibiting the spirit that moved and controlled her members in their transaction of church business, and their earnestness and single-mindedness in meeting and dealing with all matters coming before them for their consideration.

Very soon after the organization of the Church Isaac McCoy was invited to visit and preach for the church; and in the latter part of the year 1809, he removed to Maria Creek and became their regular Pastor and Moderator: filling these offices to the satisfaction of the church until some time in the year 1818, except when absent preaching as a missionary.

In Oct. 1818, he removed to Raccoon creek, in Park county, Indiana, to carry on his missionary work among the Indians. He came back to Maria Creek in April 1819, and remained some time. "During his visit there commenced," says Joseph Chambers, in a short sketch of Maria Creek Church, "the greatest ingathering, according to the number of inhabitants, ever witnessed in this country." He was assisted in this revival by Elder Aaron Frakes.

During all the time of his pastorate and ministerial labors with Maria Creek Church she steadily grew in numbers and influence, notwithstanding her location on the frontier, and consequent trials and difficulties. Sometime in 1820 he removed to Fort Wayne, Indiana, and there established a missionary school for the education of the

Indians. Schools and missionary stations were also established at Carey, on the St. Joseph river, and at Grand Rapids, on Grand River, both in the western part of Michigan.

The following extracts are taken from the History of Baptist Indian Missions, written by Isaac McCoy. While engaged in the establishment of the above mentioned schools and missionary stations he writes:

"All attempts to meliorate the condition of the Indians must prove abortive, so long as ardent spirits are freely introduced into their country. Their continued intoxication is the bane of all our efforts."

In another place he says: "The evil practice of vending liquor increased to an alarming degree. Some of our Indian converts were ensnared and became intoxicated: our religious meetings interrupted; our Indian neighbors were induced to neglect their fields and other improvements."

"The morning of the 4th of June, 1823, was memorable to me by reflections on the discouragements attending all missionary efforts for the Indians, in countries from which they soon must be driven by approaching white population. Hardly can we hope to surmount present obstacles, and do the Indians a little good before our business here must fail, by causes which we cannot control. At this time I formed the resolution that I would, Providence permitting, thence forward keep steadily in view, and endeavor to promote a plan for colonizing the natives in a country to be made forever their's, west of the State of Missouri, and from that time to the present I have considered the promotion of this as the most important business of my life."

In the prosecution of this work, Isaac McCoy spent the remainder of his life; sometimes under the patronage of the Baptist Board of Missions; sometimes employed by the Government, surveying the Indian reservations; but always urging the policy of their removal and colonization, and doing whatever he could to educate, civilize and christianize them.

The following incident, indicating the manner of man he was, was related to the writer by Joseph Chambers a short time before his death. Brother McCoy had been sick for several weeks; and when he got better he visited Brother Chambers, and in their conversation told him about how his feelings were moved, and how he was grieved the first time he visited his place of secret prayer after getting up from his sick bed. "Why," said he, "Brother Jo, the little path that led to it was all grown up with weeds."

The following extract very vividly portrays the hardships and privations to which he and his family were subjected as Missionarys among the Indians. He was at the time carrying on a missionary school at Fort Wayne, and the journey of Mrs. McCoy, he gives an account of, was from Fort Wayne to Vincennes, by canoe, down the Wabash. The incident very forcibly exhibits the courage and devotion of both Mr. and Mrs. McCoy, but especially of Mrs. McCoy. She was a brave woman, and a fit companion for a man who spent almost his whole life in laborious efforts to teach, civilize, and Christianize the Indians, and in which she was his devoted and constant helper. He says:

"The situation of Mrs. McCoy had become such as to require attention which our wilderness residence did not afford. The most eligible mode of conveying her to a suitable place in the settled country was to descend the Wabash river in an open canoe. The distance by water was between three and four hundred miles and more than half of this was through a wilderness, inhabited only by uncivilized Indians. It was the 25th of June, 1821, that, with our three younger children, she took her leave, not expecting to return in less than three months. Neither of us had ever felt a parting scene so trying as this. She was entering a gloomy desert with our three babes, and the sickly season of the year had already commenced. It was now the first of Summer, and the mosquitoes were as numerous as were ever known. The first night they encamped Mrs. McCoy spent without sleep, driving the mosquitoes from her little children. They were nine days on the river, and scarcely a day passed without rain, to which, in their open canoe, they were exposed, without shelter; their provisions damaged, and their clothing mildewed with wet and heat. Still Jacob's God was around about them by night and by day. She returned by land through the wilderness and reached Fort Wayne the 14th of September, with the addition of one to the number of her little ones. In her absence, when I was left in charge of forty-seven Indian youths, I learned by experience how onerous had been her duties when I had frequently left her sole manager of the mission."

During these early years of the church they had, besides the preaching of their pastor, occasional preaching by Elders Alexander Diven, James McQuaid, George Waller, Wm. McCoy, Wilson Thompson, and James Chambers; and up to the commencement of the year 1821 had received into her fellowship, by baptism, eighty-four; by letter, forty-eight; in all, one hundred and thirty-two members. She had become a strong church, wielding almost the entire religious influence over all the northern part of Knox county.

In 1812 Lamotte Church, in Crawford county, Illinois Territory, near where Palestine is now located, was constituted, partly by members lettered out from Maria Creek Church.

In 1817 a number of members were granted letters in order to constitute a church at Little Village, not far from where Russelville, in Illinois is now located.

In May, 1816, Prairie Creek Church, in Vigo county. Indiana, was constituted, a number of her members having obtained letters from Maria Creek Church for that purpose.

The influence of Maria Creek Church began to extend

beyond her borders in the early days of her history. And through all the eighty years of her life, has this process been going on. To-day Baptist people who once enjoyed her fellowship and communion, may be found all over the Western States and Territories.

CHAPTER III.

In 1819 the missionary controversy came up. In this controversy Maria Creek church acted a prominent part. She led the controversy in Wabash Association on the side of Missions; and Elder Daniel Parker, a member of Lamotte Church, and sustained by that church, led the other side.

Before commencing the history of the part Maria Creek Church took in that controversy, it will be proper, for its better understanding, to notice briefly the origin of Baptist missionary societies, and missionary operations in the United States.

The American Baptist Missionary Union was organized in 1814 by the advice and counsel of the older and more prominent churches and associations of the Baptist denomination. The Baptist Board of Foreign Missions was the executive Board of the Baptist Missionary Union. Numerous missionary societies auxiliary to and supporting the Missionary Union had been formed in various places. Through the Missionary Board the Baptist Missionary Union and these societies were carrying on their missionary operations; which, at that early day, consisted in translating the Bible into foreign languages, in supporting a few missionaries, (among whom was Judson), in foreign fields; and in destitute places in our own country, and among the Indians.

Prior to about the year 1818 or '19 there had been no serious opposition to these missionary operations, and no division among the Baptist on the missionary question.

All of them at least appeared to be missionary in principle, and contributed, more or less, as they were able, to the missionary cause. But about this time (1818 or '19) opposition to the Missionary Union and their executive board began among the Baptists; not only in Wabash Association, but among the Baptists all over the United States, but more especially in the West.

Among the leaders of this opposition were Daniel Parker, in the West, and Alexander Campbell, in the East. Campbell's opposition commenced three or four years later.

The parties to the controversy were called respectively, Missionary, and Anti-Missionary Baptist. There were in both parties many pious, devoted Christian men and women. Among the Anti-Missionarys these Christian men and women desired the salvation of sinners, both at home and abroad, as earnestly as the missionaries did; but were conscientiously opposed to the methods of the Baptist Board of Foreign Missions, in organizing societies and carrying on missionary work, independent, or that to them appeared to be independent, of the churches. They believed the churches, and the churches only, had authority in the matter; and that to be in Gospel order, all missionary operations ought to be under the authority and direct control of the churches; at the same time it appeared to them that the B. B. F. M. and other missionary societies acted independently, and controlled by their own authority the missionary operations, while the principal thing the churches had to do was, to furnish the money necessary to carry them on. These opinions were not altogether correct, but nevertheless they honestly entertained them, and acted accordingly. It must be observed, however, that the position occupied by these men in respect to missionary boards and societies, however honest or conscientious they may have been, naturally drew to them penurious professors of religion. It afforded them too good an excuse for refusing to give money for missionary purposes.

Their views in regard to the doctrine of Election and Predestination, in all probability, had something to do with their course in regard to missionary efforts. Believing as they did, in the doctrine of absolute election, and that God's people were all chosen in Christ from before the foundation of the world, it appeared to them that efforts to convert the world, and save sinners by means of missionary work, supported and carried on with money, were unnecessary, and in some sense a usurpation of God's prerogative; forgetting for the time, that it was as much God's prerogative to use *means* for the accomplishment of His purpose as it was to entertain the purpose itself. However this may be, I do not intend to discuss these doctrines of

Election and Predestination, only to note the fact that the anti-missionaries held them as fundamental articles of their creed; and that in all probability they were at the very foundation of their opposition to missions. While a great many of them made the distinction between principles and methods, and only intended to oppose the methods of the missionaries and not the principle of missions, the most of them failed to make the distinction, and were really what their name implied, Anti-Missionaries.

Of the missionary party it may be said that they regarded results more than methods. They saw no objections to missionary boards. They regarded them as strictly in Gospel order, and in no way inconsistent with God's sovereignty or church authority. Their anxiety for the conversion of the world inclined them to look with favor upon any method that promised success. It is to be said, however, of some of them, that they resorted to means, and used arguments, to induce people to contribute money, that were, to say the least, questionable. So it was, their differences grew more and more pronounced, bitterness came up between them, until finally they separated, and refused fellowship one with the other.

Maria Creek Church had her full share of the troubles attending this separation; and in order to give a clear and correct account she took in the controversy, it will be necessary to give some part of the history of Wabash Association.

In the year 1815, the year after the organization of the

Baptist Missionary Union, Wabash Association appointed Isaac McCoy corresponding secretary, to correspond with the Baptist Board of Foreign Missions; and in answer to said correspondence, received nine copies of the report of said board. On September 23, 1815, the following minute appears on the records of Maria Creek Church:

"The Church agrees to receive the report of the B. B. F. M. forwarded by said Board to Wabash Association for the use of the churches."

Elder McCoy was continued as corresponding secretary of the Association with the Board in 1816. The reports of the Board were received and $6.75 contributed to pay the expense of correspondence.

In 1817 the Association received a circular letter from the Board, and the following resolution appears in the minutes of the Association:

Resolved, "That this Association has received with much pleasure the above mentioned circular, and is highly pleased with the information derived therefrom."

These items from the history of Wabash Association, show its attitude towards the missionary operations of the Board prior to and during the year 1818. In that year the following query was presented to the Association by Little Village Church, of which church Daniel Parker was pastor: "Are the principles and practices of the B. B. F. M. in its present operations justifiable and agreable to Gospel order? The decision postponed until next Association." "The corresponding secretary made his report, which was cordially received. The report is a synopsis of the operations of the Foreign and Domestic Missions."

In 1819 the Association answered the query from Little Village Church as follows:

"We say they are not agreeable to Gospel order."

The correspondence with the B. B. F. M. was dropped. At the next Association in October, 1820, the following request was presented by Maria Creek Church:

"DEAR BRETHREN: United as we are in the bonds of Christian love, it is our happiness to render that respect to the Association which the wisdom and goodness of our brethren thus assembled demand. In your last minutes you informed us that the principles and practice of the B. B. F. M. were not justifiable according to Gospel order; but you omitted telling us wherein they were wrong. We do not wish any of our members to do wrong, and if it be improper for them to aid the Board of Missions, we desire to know the nature of the evils that we may endeavor to reclaim our brethren who may offend in the case. We therefore humbly request the Association to point out to us the wickedness of the B. B. F. M., and it will be our happiness to avoid everything which we conceive contrary to the mind and will of Christ."

The Association answers:

"We hope no use will be made of the decision of last Association relative to the subject of missions, to the distress of Zion, contrary to the commands of Christ."

Patoka Church also asked advice "in cases where the

principles and practice of the B. B. F. M. are cherished and nourished among us." Answer: "We advise the churches to cherish brotherly love, and to walk in all the commands of Christ blameless."

Sometime during this year (1820) Elder Daniel Parker published a pamphlet giving his views on the subject of missionary operations, which gave rise to the following charges against him, presented to Lamotte Church by Maria Creek Church:

"Oct. 14, 1820. Church met and proceeded to business.

"Bro. Wm. Polke moved that members be appointed to go to Lamotte Church and lay in a complaint to said church against Elder Daniel Parker, and stated the following charges against him, which he says he can support:

"1st. He has publically accused many of his brethren with fraud, falsehood and intrigue, without taking Gospel steps with those whom he accuses. See page 12 of his address on missions.

"2d. He has said the counsel of the union is neither asked nor known in the mission plan, (see page 52) when we believe he knew the counsel of the union had been asked more than once. We say we believe he knew this, for on the 19th page of his book he refers us to the 234th page of the Latter Day Luminary, so that we believe he had read that very page, and the 7th resolve of said page requests the sentiments of the ministers and churches of the Baptist denomination to be forwarded to the Board of Missions. Also, in a printed circular read in presence of

Bro Parker at Wabash Association in 1819, the advice of the denomination is asked. We believe Brother Parker knew that the advice of the union had been asked in both these instances, and yet he says it is neither asked nor known.

"3d. He says the B. B. F. M. believe education essential to the Gospel ministry, when the Board of Missions on the 240th page of the same number of the Luminary, to which he refers us, says they do not. Their words are, 'That as there are at present, so there ever will be many useful and able ministers who never enjoyed the advantages of any public institution whatever.' See also third annual report, page 128, where they say, they are fully sensible that in relation to grace in the heart a sacred necessity compelling to the work, and a valuable success that shall accompany pulpit labor, the Lord alone can make able ministers of the New Testament.

"4th. He also says on page 53, our brethren have gone astray, they have sinned against the King of Zion, they have violated our government and thereby forfeited their right to the Baptist Union, for they have left us."

"The church, after hearing the above motion, refer the decision to the next meeting."

"Nov. 18th. Church met. The reference from last meeting acted upon. Whereupon Brethren Wm. Polke, Joseph Chambers, Thomas Piety, Sam'l Lemen and Jesse Haddon, were appointed a committee to wait on Lamotte Church with the foregoing charges against Brother Parker, and endeavor to obtain satisfaction, and bear with them the letter this day read by the clerk and approved by the church."

"Feb. 17, 1821. The members appointed at our last November meeting to bear a letter to Lamotte Church informing them of our distress with a member of Lamotte Church, to-wit: Elder Daniel Parker, informed the church that they had performed that service, and received from Lamotte Church the following answer: Lamotte Church to her sister church at Maria Creek:

"DEAR BRETHREN: There has this day been a letter presented to us by members of your body, which we understand contained charges against a member of our body; and we are sorry to have to say, we did not admit it to be read, because in our judgment the legal Gospel steps had not been taken; but we are ready to receive a charge against any of our members when brought in Gospel order. These are the reasons that we have returned your letter by the hands of your messengers. Done in conference at our monthly meeting, Feb. 10th. 1821. Signed by order of the church. W. M. RYAN, Clerk."

"March 17, 1821. Elder Thomas Kennedy, a member from Lamotte Church, informed the church that he was authorized by Elder Daniel Parker to say: If the church had not passed any resolutions respecting the unhappy difficulty existing between this church and Bro. Parker, that he, Bro. Parker, would endeavor to attend our next meeting, when he thought such measures might be adopted as would settle the business, he hoped, to the satisfaction of both parties."

"April 14th, 1821. Elder Daniel Parker presented a charge in writing to this church, of which the following is a copy:

"I am grieved with my Brethren, Wm. Polke and Joseph Chambers, because I view they have sinned in joining with and supporting of the principle and practice of what is called the Baptist Board of Foreign Missions, which principle and practice I view a departing from the Gospel and general principle and practice of the Baptist Union."

The church did not receive the above charge. Elder Parker offered the following charge:

"I feel I have cause of grief in consequence of the illegal proceedings of Maria Creek Church in her manner of dealing with me."

The church did not receive this charge.

"Bro. Parker requested an opportunity of giving some explanation relative to the subjects on which the charges against him are grounded. On motion, liberty was given.

"The church received no satisfaction from Bro. Parker's explanation of the first charge; nor did his explanation of the second, third and fourth charges give satisfaction.

"Further proceedings on the subject were postponed until next meeting."

"May 19th, 1821. The reference from last meeting respecting the difficulty existing between Maria Creek and Lamotte churches, in respect to the charges against Elder Daniel Parker, taken up and considered. The church agrees to refer all further proceeding until after the next association, and request the advice of the association on the point of discipline in dispute between the churches, and the clerk is directed to furnish copies of all papers and records of the church connected with or relating thereto, to our messengers to the next association to be by them laid before that body if necessary."

"Brother Thomas Kennedy, from Lamotte Church, handed to the clerk the following letter from that church:

"The Baptist Church at Lamotte to her sister church at Maria Creek:

"DEAR BRETHREN: We think we have in view the close union that should exist in the body of Christ, and under a sense of you and us being members of that Body and thus united in one bond, we should possess as it were the heart of one man; and when we feel to esteem this union so great, sweet and pleasant to our souls, it is a heart rending thought to us to be under the necessity to inform you that in several parts of your conduct as a church, you have given great wounds to our feelings; and we now apply to you hoping you will give us satisfaction. We are grieved with you in the following parts of your conduct. First, In your refusing to receive the charges offered to you in Gospel order by a member of our body, to-wit: Elder Daniel Parker, against two members of your body, to-wit: Wm. Polke and Joseph Chambers for holding and supporting the principle and practice of what is called the Baptist Board of Foreign Missions. This act of your's more fully proves to us that you as a church do hold and justify that principle, which is the cause of our second hurt with you, and we have to say to you, this is our great grief that you hold the principle and justify the practice of the Baptist Board of Foreign Missions, so far as to justify your members in supporting it. This principle we view as heterodox, and the practice not justifiable by Gospel authority and discipline. In the third place we are grieved with you because you refused to hear the complaint of Brother Daniel Parker, a member of our body, which he offered against you for your improper course of dealing with him. In the fourth place our grief is that you still hold the charges against him that are not only improperly taken up, but by the best information that we have got, are unjust in their nature. So, dear brethren, we hope you will be disposed to remove the cause of grief and give us satisfaction. We send this by our Brethren, Thomas Kennedy, William Hearn, James Ryan, and Benjamin Parker, whom we authorize to transact our business with you in this case, and we pray the Great Head of the Church to interfere in our behalf, and preserve his body from the apparent distress and the cause of Zion from reproach. Yours in the bonds of the Gospel. Done in conference at our meeting of business, May the 12th, 1821.

WM. RYAN, Clerk."

"The members mentioned in the foregoing letter, all were present.

"The church, after hearing the above complaint, and hearing the brethren on each charge contained therein, justify her conduct in her proceeding in relation to her conduct with Elder Daniel Parker."

"On motion the clerk directed to prepare a friendly letter to Lamotte Church, informing them of the decision of this church, and present the same to the church on to-morrow morning."

"Sunday morning. The clerk produced and read the following letter to Lamotte church, which, being approved was handed to Bro. Thos. Kennedy, with a request that he would lay the same before Lamotte Church."

"The Baptist church at Maria Creek, Knox Co., State of Indiana, to her Sister Church at Lamotte, Crawford Co., State of Illinois: Sendeth Christian salutation:

DEAR BRETHREN: We received your letter by the hands of your messengers, Thos. Kennedy, Wm. Hearn, James Ryan and Benjamin Parker, exhibiting charges against us in regard to our not receiving the charges which one of your members, to-wit: Daniel Parker, presented to this church against two of her members, to-wit: Brethren Joseph Chambers and Wm. Polke, for holding and supporting the principles and practice of the Baptist Board of Foreign Missions, and in reply we have to observe, that Maria Creek Church have, by her correspondence to the Association, manifested and declared she approved of missionary efforts, as patronized by the Baptist Board of Foreign Missions, and as we have, on all occasions, publicly announced that we approved of missions, we could not consistently receive charges against any of our individual members; and as we are still of the same opinion, we cannot make any acknowledgements in replying to the

foregoing charge. We have given you our opinion on the second charge. In reply to your third charge we are fully persuaded that we acted correctly in our mode of proceeding in respect to our charges against Elder Daniel Parker, and of course cannot make any acknowledgements. In your fourth and last charge you complain of our still holding the charges against your member, and hint that you believe them to be unjust in their nature from the best information you have. We cannot but regret that you had not fully informed yourselves of the nature of our charges against the offending brother, before you had hastily condemned us in this indirect manner, and we have to repeat to you that we believe we have acted agreeably to the discipline laid down in the Gospel; and we further say that we believe we can fully support our charges before any competent tribunal. With you we lament the difficulties that exist between us; and join with you in praying Zion's King that He will take care of His church, avert the threatening evils, and that He will show us our errors and restore harmony and union between us. With these sentiments we remain yours in the bonds of the Gospel.   JOSEPH CHAMBERS, Mod.
  WM. POLKE, Clerk."

"July 13th, 1821. A door being opened, the members appointed by Lamotte Church presented her charges against Maria Creek Church, having called in the assistance of Prairie Creek and Little Village Churches. The charges the same as laid in at last May meeting by letter from Lamotte Church.

"After consideration of the first charge the church on motion decided that she was justifiable in refusing to hear Elder Daniel Parker's charge against Brethren Joseph Chambers and Wm. Polke.

"Second charge. The Maria Creek Church holds the principles and practice of the Board of Foreign Missions. After considering the charge, the church, on motion says she has no acknowledgments to make to Lamotte church as to any part of said charge.

"Third charge. We are grieved with you because you refused to hear the complaint of Brother Daniel Parker, a member of our body, offered against you for your improper course in dealing with him.

"The messengers from Lamotte Church withdrew the foregoing charge in consequence of Maria Creek Church having submitted the point of discipline in dispute between the two churches, to the next Association, and postponed all further proceeding thereon until the advice of the association can be obtained.

"Fourth charge. Our grief is that you still held the charges against him (Bro. Parker) that are not only improperly taken up, but by the best information that we have, are unjust in their nature.

"The Messengers from Lamotte Church agree to drop any further investigation of the fourth charge until after the association."

A letter was read by the messengers from Lamotte Church proposing a reconciliation in the following words:

"The Baptist Church of Christ at Lamotte to her sister church at Maria Creek, Greeting:

Dear Brethren: It is painful to us to anticipate any thing like a division in the Body of Christ; and when we take a view of the difficulties that are now existing between us, we feel so sensibly that our brethren have departed from the order of the Gospel, that we are constrained to believe a division must take place, unless prevented by the Head of the Church leading our minds into some way that may be agreeable to Gospel order, and meet the approbation of the union.

"Dear Brethren, we would be willing to do anything consistent with the Gospel for the preservation of the union, and to prevent the breaches which appear to be impending; and we believe that there is a way whereby the children of God may unite in harmony in the management of the affairs of His Kingdom, and that it may be found in Gospel order by a close attention thereto. You say that you think it is a duty to educate the Indians and translate the Scriptures into the languages of nations which are destitute of the light of Revelation. We also believe it is a duty, and thus far we are agreed, and we do not wish to hinder you from doing that which you and us believe to be our duty, but would willingly unite with you in a way consistent with the Gospel to accomplish the object, and the best way that we can see to expedite the business is to submit it to the direction and government of the union; as it is a work that will require the united strength of the whole denomination.

"If we undertake to form plans for the union we shall be sure to err and procrastinate the work, for it is a right that does belong to the Church of Christ, whilst conducted under its name, and it is an error to assume a right or authority which does not belong to us, and we cannot expect that the church will give up her right which may now be plainly seen in respect to the plan of the general convention of the missionary societies. Then for us to formulate plans would be to retard the work instead of facilitating it. But we are willing to unite with you heart and hand in submitting it to the direction and government of the Baptist Union, and to do all we can to accomplish the object.

"We have no doubt but there are other exertions besides translating the Bible and educating the heathen that are incumbent on Christians. Let them be attended to by the direction and under the government of the union and we have no objections, but are perfectly willing to unite therein. We think this looks like the way to preserve the union, and in this way we are willing to meet and unite with you in the work. But we cannot consent to any system or establishments that are not by the advice and under the government of the church in matters of so great a magnitude. And we do think that if you will seriously reflect on the nature of the union of Christ's Body, that you must see that the setting up religious institutions distinct from the union, is the very way to split the union, and we trust and hope you will see that the measures we are pursuing toward you are not designed to split the union; but, we trust, are calculated to preserve the Gospel order, and the union of the Church of Christ. And now, dear brethren, if you are willing to unite with us in this way, a moment's reflection will show how the voice of the union is to be obtained; and we are willing to join you in counsel to accomplish this object. Dear Brethren, may the Lord guide all our minds into the way that is right in His sight, and restore peace and harmony to His people. is the prayer of yours in Gospel bonds. Done in conference July 7th, 1821. WM. PATRICK, Clerk."

"On motion, agreed to accede to the proposition from Lamotte Church for a reconciliation on condition that Maria Creek Church and her members individually be permitted to pursue her present Missionary pursuits until a plan can be brought into operation that may be approved of by a majority of the Baptist Union, which was unanimously adopted, and agreed to by the messengers from Lamotte Church. Whereupon the clerk was, on motion, directed to prepare a letter to send to Lamotte Church, informing them of the terms on which we accede to their propositions; and for the purpose of bringing about a reconciliation."

"On the 4th of August the following letter was approved by the church, and Brethren Levi Chambers, Jesse

Hollingsworth and Wm. Polke, appointed to bear the same to Lamotte Church.

"The Baptist Church of Jesus Christ at Maria Creek, Knox Co., Indiana, to her sister Church at Lamotte, Crawford Co., Illinois, sendeth Christian salutation.

"DEAR BRETHREN: We with pleasure received your letter of July the 7th, 1821, by the hands of Elder Daniel Parker and others, members of your church, appointed a committeteo bear the same and transact other business with us, containing, or amounting to terms of reconciliation in respect to the unpleasant difficulties that exist between us; and we truly rejoice to find that our brethren are not opposed to making use of such exertions as God in His providence may enable them to do, to aid in giving the Scriptures and a knowledge of civilized life to the ignorant and wretched of all nations; provided the same can be done consistent with the Gospel, and under the direction and government of the Baptist Union. Notwithstanding we were highly gratified with these sentiments, it was with regret we found that you had so condemned the present missionary operations of the Baptist Board of Foreign Missions in the United States, in which we are engaged, as precluded all hopes of a reconciliation or adjustment of our difficulties previous to our abandoning our present missionary pursuits; which we fully believe has been blessed of God to the extension of the visible church here on earth; is not inconsistent with the Gospel; and in no wise incompatible with the Baptist Union, or power, or privileges of the Church of Jesus Christ. But being desirous to have the unhappy difficulties existing between us adjusted as soon as practicable, and finding we only differed as to the means employed to accomplish the same ends; and believing it our duty to use all reasonable means to give our brethren satisfaction, a proposal was made on the part of Maria Creek Church to your committee, who, we were informed by an extract from your minutes, were by you fully authorized to transact your business with us; that Maria Creek Church and her members individually should be permitted to pursue without molestation her present missionary pursuits, until a plan can be so matured, approved of and carried into active operation, as shall be accepted by a majority of the churches composing the Baptist union in the United States, for the purpose of translating the Scriptures, educating the heathen and such other exertions as may be thought necessary, under the smiles of our God, to accomplish the great and benevolent purposes of putting the word of life into the hands of all nations under the sun; which proposition was unanimously acceeded to by your committee; and in order to bring about as speedy and happy an intercourse as practicable, and restore that harmony which to us is so desirable, we send you this by the hands of our Brethren, Levi Chambers, Jesse Hollingsworth and Wm. Polke, as a manifestation of our Christian love and friendship; hoping we may bring the subject before the churches in such a way as may unite all Christians in the noble work of sending the Scriptures to all the families of the earth; and that Zion's Prophet, Priest and King, may, by His Holy Spirit and Grace, guide us into all truth, is the prayer of yours in Gospel bonds.

WM. POLKE, Clerk."

"August 18th, 1821. The following letter received from Lamotte Church by the hands of Brethren, Jesse Hollingsworth and Levi Chambers who attended Lamotte Church at her last meeting with our letter to said church."

"We, the Baptist Church of Christ at Lamotte, to her sister church at Maria Creek, sendeth Christian salutation:

"DEAR BRETHREN: Received your letter by Brethren Jesse Hollingsworth and Levi Chambers, and we are very much gratified to hear that you are yet willing to strive for peace. But still we believe there is a misunderstanding between us as respects your limitation in your pursuits in missionary efforts. You stated in your letter that you were to pursue your present engagements in missionary efforts until the counsel of the union should be known and a better plan should be carried into active operation. Our understanding of the proposition made by you was, that you should pursue your present missionary efforts until the voice of the union should be known; and then you were to relinquish or forsake such parts as they should in their wisdom deem unjustifiable. And we are sorry to say that there is another point in which we do not understand one another. We do not think we are bound to wait until the voice of the whole denomination should be known. If we should agree to wait until a final decision of the whole denomination, it would be in our opinion, impracticable. For if we were to give you latitude without molestation to proceed in your mission efforts until that should be the case, we are entirely done, and had as well say, go on until you should see cause to desist yourselves. Now, dear brethren, our opinion, in a few words, amounts to about this: We believe our association is the beginning and after we have laid our plan before the Wabash Association, and they should approve of it, so far as to submit it to the churches and they should approve of it, it will then continue its process as far as practicable. But if they should disapprove of it, we are then done; for we have no legal way of introducing it in any other association, except the one in which we have our membership. Dear brethren, notwithstanding the seeming difficulties that appear to exist, we are willing to meet you at your September meeting, for the purpose of devising a plan upon which we can all unite, and perhaps by that time we can see some way whereby it can be submitted to other associations in legal form. And may the Lord in His infinite mercy and unbounded wisdom, direct us in a way that shall be for the promotion of the Redeemer's Kingdom, and the salvation of our immortal souls hereafter, is the prayer of yours in Gospel bonds. Done at our meeting of business on Saturday, the 11th of August, 1821, and signed by order of the church. WM. PATRICK, Clerk."

"Sept. 15th, 1821. Received the following letter from Lamotte church:

"The Church of Jesus Christ at Lamotte, Crawford Co., Illinois, to her Sister Church at Maria Creek, Knox Co., Indiana, sendeth Christian salutation:

"DEAR BRETHREN: According to our promise we have appointed our Brethren Daniel Parker, Thomas Kennedy, and Wm. Patrick, a committee to transact our business with you in the compromise which was proposed by us to you, and to which in your letter of August the 4th you manifested something of a disposition to accede; but as your propositions do not meet our views, and still hoping our difficulties may be adjusted to satisfaction, we think it necessary to state plainly to you what we wish, and what we are willing to do, and that which we think is plainly implied in our letter of compromise. First, we have let you know that we believe that translating the Scriptures, and educating the heathen are things that are laudable and right, and that we believe there are other duties which are incumbent on Christians; but as we discover there are different sentiments among the Baptists in regard to what ought to be done, we think it ought to be referred to the union to say what is right or is not right to be done. Secondly, when the work is of so much magnitude as to require the united strength of our brethren, we think it ought to be submitted to the union, to prescribe the plan, and the whole be conducted under the government of the union. And now, dear brethren we think we plainly stated what we are willing to submit to, and what we want you to submit to, and if you comply with these propositions, we feel hopeful that our difficulties may be amicably adjusted, as we are willing to bear with you in your present missionary pursuits until the voice of the union can be known, and so far as they may be justified by the union, until a plan can be adopted and be carried into active operation by the union. With respect to the union, you have stated in your proposition contained in your letter, that Maria Creek Church, and her members individually, should be permitted to pursue unmolested, their present missionary efforts, until a plan can be matured, approved, and carried into active operation by a majority of the churches, composing the Baptist Union in America. To this proposition we cannot accede. It would be, in our opinion, to violate the principles and rules of our own union, and lest there should be some mistake, will tell you plainly; 1st, what we mean when we say, bring it to the union; 2d, the course to pursue; 3d, how far we can indulge you.

First. When we say bring it to the Union, we mean the churches composing the Wabash Association; as that is all the place that we, as churches, can come.

Second. When a plan is formed by the churches in our association, it can be formed in a way to progress by the way of our correspondence with our sister associations, and so on, and at the same time the whole procedure subject to be changed as it progresses under the direction and government of the Baptist denomination.

Third. We are willing to indulge you where you are, until we can get the counsel of the churches in our association, and whatever they say is right for us to do we will submit to pursue, and you submit to the same; and when a plan is formed by the counsel of the churches, and under their government, you and us be governed by the direction of the union. We then have no right to say anything more, as to your indulgence, for if the union say stop, or come out from where you are, you must obey, and if they say go on, we must submit. But as an individual church we can assure you from our present impressions, that we shall not be in favor of leaving those that are engaged in printing, or in teaching the heathen, to suffer. If they will come under our government, we would either bring them home or support them there.

"Now, Dear Brethren, we think this is a plain, a fair way, easy to be understood, and if you are disposed to meet us in this way we can rejoice in peace between us, and have authorized our committee to join with you in counsel to devise and pursue measures to bring the matter fairly and legally before the union, in order to obtain the voice thereof, and carry our desires into active operation. But if you will not accede to these propositions, we have to say with pain, we shall be under the necessity of desisting from an expectation of adjusting our difficulties by way of compromise.

"May the God of all grace be with you and guide you and us unto all truth, is the prayer of yours in Gospel bonds. Signed by order of the church at her meeting of business, September 8th, 1821.

WILLIAM PATRICK, Clerk."

"Oct. 4th, 1821. Maria Creek Church sent the following response to the above letter:

"The Church of Jesus Christ at Maria Creek, Knox Co., Ind., to her sister church at Lamotte, Crawford Co., Ills., greeting:

"DEAR BRETHREN: Your letter of September 8th, 1821, was received, wherein you explain what your views of the union are, and the nature of the compromise entered into at our July meeting, between Maria Creek Church and a committee of Lamotte Church, authorized by an act of Lamotte Church, to transact her business with us. We still believe we correctly understood the terms of compromise, and are willing to abide by the terms as understood by us, and which your letter of compromise will show was correct. But should you still differ with us, you can act as you think proper, as we conceive no good will result from any further attempt to settle the difficulties existing between us. May the Lord by His Spirit guide us into all truth, is the prayer of yours in Gospel bonds. Done by order of the church at special meeting of business, Thursday, October the 4th, 1821.

WM. POLKE, Clerk."

"March 16th, 1822. Elder Daniel Parker from Lamotte Church handed in the following letter:

"The Baptist Church of Christ at Lamotte, to her sister church at Maria Creek, sendeth greetings:

DEAR BRETHREN: Although your last letter to us was calculated to discourage any further attempts to settle or compromise the difficulty between us, but still desirous to be at peace with our brethren, and not to be weary in well-doing, we therefore, on the encouragement given us by Brother Wm. Polke, we feel it our duty to make one more attempt for peace. We have taken into consideration the statement of Brother Polke in our last association, when he was remarking on the subject of missions, and as it respected the difficulty on that point, his statement was about in these words: 'All we want is liberty to give our mite, an Indian a Bible, a shirt or something like this.' And as he was acting by the authority of your church in the association, we are led to hope for peace, for we are unanimously agreed that you shall fully and freely have all that request, for this you can do without pursuing the course where we think the sin lies. And now, dear brethren, this is what will satisfy us: For you to cause your members to forsake and quit their connection with the Baptist Board of Foreign Missions, and on these principles we both can have our desires without interfering with each other's feelings. And for this purpose we appoint our Brethren Elder Daniel Parker, Wm. Hearn and William Patrick to compromise with you upon the above stated terms, and do fully authorize them to act on our part. Signed by order of the church, March 19, 1822.

        WM. PATRICK, Clerk."

To this letter Maria Creek Church returned the following answer:

"The Baptist Church of Jesus Christ at Maria Creek, Knox Co., Ind., to her sister church at Lamotte, greeting:

DEAR BRETHREN: Your letter to us was received by the hands of Elder Daniel Parker, Brethren Wm. Hearn and Wm. Patrick, in which you state that one of our members, Bro. Wm. Polke, at our last Association made an observation to the following amount, to-wit: 'All we want is liberty to give our mite, an Indian a Bible, a shirt or something like this,' in which explanation we are happy to say, our brother justly represented our views; and as your letter stated you were willing we should have these privileges, we were much gratified on hearing these statements, as we were in hopes a happy reconciliation would ensue. But on perusing your letter further wherein you state on what terms we may pursue our missionary efforts, these hopes expired. As you state that we must cause our members to forsake and quit their connection with the Baptist Board of Foreign Missions, and as we only make use of the Baptist Board of Foreign Missions as a medium whereby to communicate our liberality, we cannot prohibit our members from their connection with the board, as we retain our sentiments on that subject heretofore expressed in our correspondence with you. And that the Lord may guide us into all truth is the prayer of yours in Gospel Bonds. Signed by order of the church.

WM. POLKE, Clerk.

———o———

CHAPTER IV.

The letter at the conclusion of the last chapter ended the correspondence of Maria Creek and Lamotte churches upon the subject of Missions. There was some further correspondence between them, which will now be noticed; after which the further history of the controversy on missions will be resumed.

It will be remembered that when Maria Creek Church presented charges against Daniel Parker, before Lamotte Church, of which body Elder Parker was a member, that Lamotte Church refused to consider them, on the ground that Gospel steps had not been taken, thus raising a question of discipline between the two churches. This question of discipline was afterwards referred by Maria Creek Church to the association, and decided by that body at their special meeting, at Patoka, on the 8th of June, 1822. Maria Creek Church accepted that decision, and in accord with it, on the 15th of June, 1822, appointed Brethren Wm. Polke, Joseph Chambers and Wm. Bruce, a committee to labor with Elder Daniel Parker, a member of

Lamotte Church, and if satisfaction is not obtained, to lay the matter before Lamotte Church. This committee visited Lamotte Church, and upon their return Wm. Polke made the following report:

"Sept. 14th, 1822. Agreeably to the appointment of the church I, in company with Brother Wm. Bruce, attended Lamotte Church at her last meeting, and on conversing with Elder Daniel Parker and Thomas Kennedy, on the subject of the charges against Elder Daniel Parker, was informed by them that Lamotte Church would not receive or hear a charge on behalf of Maria Creek Church. I then presented said charges in my own name and on my own individual responsibility, and on Lamotte Church hearing said charges, and Elder Daniel Parker's defense, in which he justified himself in the statements in his book, complained of, acquitted him of blame."

"On motion, the church approved of the course Brother Polke has taken, and discontinue the charges against Elder Daniel Parker."

"On motion, the church say they will take Gospel steps with Lamotte Church."

This resolution was reconsidered on Nov. 16th, 1822, "When the church agreed to discontinue any further proceeding, as we believe no good will result from pursuing the subject farther. But at the same time believe we have acted correctly, and there is cause of grief in the charges that have been preferred against a member of Lamotte Church."

Prior to this last action of Maria Creek Church, to-wit:

On July 20, 1822, the following letter was received from Lamotte Church:

"State of Illinois, Crawford Co.

"The Baptist Church of Christ at Lamotte, to her sister church at Maria Creek, sendeth greeting:

DEAR BRETHREN: We are sorry to find that there is still cause of grief between us. We find from the statement of your letter, written to us in August, 1821, and by the information of our committee that attended your meeting in September, that you have on your record, that there was an agreement entered into by you and our committee that attended you in July, 1821, to this amount: That your members were permitted to pursue their mission course unmolested until the voice of the Baptist denomination in America should be taken. We are informed by our committee that attended you at that time, that your record is certainly incorrect; and consequently we are grieved with you in this case; and when we have heard the use that you or your members are making of this record of yours, we are still worse hurt. So, Brethren, we hope you will take this matter under consideration and give us relief. We have appointed Elder Thomas Kennedy and Brethren Wm. Hearn and Wm. Patrick to hand you this and attend to our business with you. And may the Lord direct you and us, and remove iniquity from Zion and restore peace to Israel, is the prayer of yours in Gospel bonds. Done at our meeting of business and signed by order of the church, July the 12th, 1822. WILLIAM PATRICK, Clerk."

To this letter Maria Creek Church answers:

"The Baptist Church of Jesus Christ at Maria Creek, Knox Co., Ind., to her sister church at Lamotte, Crawford Co., Illinois, greeting:

DEAR BRETHREN: We are fully pursuaded that the minutes of our July meeting, 1821, (referred to in your letter to us of the 12th instant) are correct. Yours in Gospel bonds. By order of the church at her meeting of business on Saturday, July the 20th, 1822. WM. POLKE, Clk."

This charge against Maria Creek Church, of making a false record, was afterwards submitted by agreement of both churches to a committee of referees, consisting of Thomas Pound, Philip Frakes, Robert Davidson and Wm. Pound from Prairie Creek Church, Samuel Baker from Little Village Church, Wm. Welsh from Union Church and Robt. Elliott from Wabash Church.

The committee, after hearing all the evidence from both churches, and fully investigating the matter, rendered the following decision:

"We the committee are of opinion that Maria Creek Church was justifiable in making the record as she did; as the committee from Lamotte Church did not let Maria Creek Church know that they had laid down their authority from Lamotte Church."

Thus ended all matter of controversy directly between Lamotte and Maria Creek churches.

We now go back and resume the history of the missionary controversy, and in doing so it will be necessary to refer again to the history of Wabash Association. The controversy between Maria Creek and Lamotte churches was transferred to that body.

At the meeting of the association in October, 1821, at Lamotte Church, a proposition to change its constitution was submitted. The constitution provided that questions coming before the association from the churches should be decided by a majority vote of the association. It was proposed to amend this provision of the constitution; the amendment providing that questions from the churches coming before the association for advice or decision should be "referred by that body to the churches, to be voted upon by each church in the association, and the result reported at the next meeting of the association, and the vote of a majority of all the churches to constitute a decision."

This proposition to amend the constitution was referred to the churches, and a special association called to meet in June, 1822, to ascertain the voice of the churches in regard to the proposed amendment. Accordingly the association met at Patoka Church, on the 8th of June, 1822, when it appeared that a majority of the churches sanctioned the proposed change. The matter was then referred to the regular meeting of the association, which was to convene in October, 1822, at Prairie Creek Church in Vigo county.

At this special meeting, in June, of the association,

Lamotte Church presented the following charges against Maria Creek Church, to-wit: "1st. She refused to receive and act on charges legally exhibited by a member of our body against two members of her body. 2d. For holding to and justifying her members in the support of the principles and practice of the Baptist Board of Foreign Missions, which principles, so far as connected with the ministry, we believe to be hetrodox; and we also believe the practice in every respect, while practiced under the name of the Baptist, and at the same time is in no legal way under the government of the Baptist Union. And we also believe that both the principles and practice are contrary to the principles of our union."

After investigation and due consideration of these charges, the association dismissed them.

The regular meeting of the association convened at Prairie Creek, October 5th, 1822. In the mean time all the churches south of White river had organized Salem Association; so that of the twenty-one churches composing the Wabash Association, in 1821, only twelve remained in 1822.

Lamotte Church again presented the same charges against Maria Creek Church that had been presented and dismissed at the special meeting in June. These charges were now, according to the amended constitution, referred to the churches for trial and investigation by each church, and the decision of each to be forwarded to the next association, a majority of all constituting a decision. At the special meeting in June, Maria Creek Church had met the charges and defended herself before the association, and that body had dismissed them. But now when these same charges were renewed and referred to the churches she was deprived of the power of making any defense whatever, as she could not know when the different churches would act on these charges, unless notified by them, which the churches, especially those opposed to Maria Creek Church, being in no way legally bound, would not be very likely to do.

The next association met at Maria Creek Church, Oct. 6th, 1823. Elders Moses Pearson, Samuel Anderson and Royce McCoy, were appointed a committee to examine the letters from the churches composing the association and report their decision upon the charges against Maria Creek Church, which had been referred to the churches by the last association. The committee reported as follows: Two churches decided that the mission cause was no bar to fellowship; two churches justified Maria Creek Church; one church was neutral and five churches sustained the charges against Maria Creek Church. Lamotte and Maria Creek churches not voting. Upon this report a discussion arose between Daniel Parker and the delegates from Maria Creek Church. Parker contending that the vote sustained the charges; and the delegates from Maria Creek Church contending that it did not; as only five churches of the twelve had decided against Maria Creek Church, which was not a majority. Pending this discussion, a proposition was made and a committee appointed to divide the association, as they could not walk together in harmony. This committee, consisting of Brethren John Parker, Thomas Pound, Asa Norton, Robert Elliott and Daniel Parker, reported in favor of a division; and that each church should choose whether she would remain in Wabash Association or go into a new association, to be organized the next year, which report was adopted. The division of the association was consummated the next year; the anti-missionary churches remaining in Wabash Association, and the missionary churches, to-wit: Wabash, Maria Creek, Little Flock, Busseron, Union, Veals Creek and Boggs Creek churches, meeting by delegates with Little Flock Church, on Curry's Prairie, on Saturday before the Third Sunday in September, 1824, and organized Union Association.

Thus ended the controversy on missions between the churches of Wabash Association. Maria Creek Church and Lamotte Church were the leaders in this controversy. It will be seen by a close attention to the correspondence between these churches, and the conduct of Maria Creek Church in the association, that Maria Creek Church was consistent throughout the controversy. She maintained her dignity and boldly contended for the principles she professed and conscientiously believed, marching straightforward, without wavering in the discharge of what she believed to be her duty. When we remember that during the greater part of the time that this controversy was going on she was without a pastor, Isaac McCoy, her first pastor having gone as a missionary to the Indians, and Aaron Frakes, who succeeded him, having died on the 23d of February, 1821, almost at the beginning of the controversy, we cannot but respect and honor the members who were prominent in thus contending for their principles, and the whole church that so cordially sustained and encouraged them.

The controversy was now transferred to, and went on between the associations. At the time Wabash Association was divided in 1823, it was claimed by Daniel Parker that a majority of the churches that voted upon the charges against Maria Creek Church had voted to sustain said charges, and accordingly in the minutes of that year Maria Creek Church was published as excluded from Wabash Association, although there was no vote upon her exclusion, but a vote to divide the association. All the missionary churches were as much excluded as Maria Creek Church. When Union Association was organized the next year, she petitioned for correspondence with Wabash Association, but was refused because she had admitted Maria Creek Church as a member, which Church Wabash Association considered in disorder, and had published her as excluded for justifying her members in their support of the Baptist Board of Foreign Missions.

At the time of her pretended exclusion in 1823, Elder Tyra Harris, a member of Little Flock Church was appointed to preach the introductory sermon at the next meeting of Wabash Association. This he was not permitted to do, Elder Daniel Parker objecting on the ground that Little Flock Church had gone into the Union Association with Maria Creek Church; which objection was sustained by Wabash Association.

The following resolution appears in her minutes of that year (1824):

"*Resolved*, That we recommend to the churches to set apart a portion of their time for prayer for the outpouring of the Holy Spirit and for the *spread of the Gospel.*"

At the meeting of Wabash Association in 1825 she refused correspondence with Salem Association, because she (Salem Association) corresponded with Union Association, and White River, Blue River and Highland associations, all dropped correspondence with Wabash Association, because she had excluded Maria Creek Church.

Wabash Association passed the following resolution:

"WHEREAS, The churches composing the Wabash Association having determined that supporting the principles and practice of the Baptist Board of Foreign Missions, is a deviation from the Baptist faith, as well as the true order of the Gospel of Christ, they feel it a duty to make it a bar to fellowship.

Resolved, Therefore, that as Maria Creek Church has been excluded by an act of the churches composing this body for holding to and justifying the principles and practices of said board; and failing to give satisfaction to their grieved brethren; and as the Union Association has, regardless of the fellowship of their brethren, as well as the order of the Gospel discipline, in the face of all these facts, received said church into her body; that we now write to White River, Blue River and Salem associations and inform them that as they have opened a correspondence with the Union Association, to the support of their disorder, as well as the mission system, that under these circumstances our church fellowship and correspondence, both directly and indirectly, are now dissolved."

The controversy between the churches and associations now ceased so far as any action of these bodies were concerned. But it went on among the people, the ministers and lay members of each party contending that they were right and the other party wrong. But time has, in great measure, decided the question; and if time be a righteous judge, Maria Creek Church stands before the world fully justified.

———o———

CHAPTER V.

In 1821 Maria Creek Church had so increased in numbers that the log cabin was too small to accommodate her meetings. Accordingly they proceeded to erect a more commodious house.

"Sept., 1822. The committee appointed last meeting on the subject of the meeting house, made the following report, which was adopted:

"Sept. 28th, 1822. We the undersigned, appointed a committee to converse with Brother Samuel Lemen, respecting a site on which to build a meeting house, and to suggest a plan for a building, beg leave to report as follows:

"Brother Samuel Lemen proposes to let the church have one acre of ground at Five Dollars, located so as to include the creek and a spring, and a sufficiency of high ground to build on. Also Brother Jonathan Cox proposes to let the church have one-half acre adjoining the tract proposed by Brother Lemen, at the price of Two Dollars and Fifty cents.

"We also recommend a brick building 30 by 45 feet. We have made a rough calculation of the cost and are of opinion that a house one story high, that is, 12 feet above ground, have it put under cover, with plank for the floor and doors, and windows can be built for $450.00. We further recommend that the expenses of the same be raised by assessment of the members. But we wish it to be distinctly understood that no person shall be assessed who has conscientious scruples as to that mode of procedure. Accordingly a committee was appointed to superintend the building, trustees were elected, and a title to the ground secured, and the building erected. The location of this house was on the bank of Maria Creek near the present crossing of the Oaktown road.

After the revival in 1819-20, already mentioned, in which Elder Aaron Frakes was engaged, he continued to visit the church occasionally and preach for them. In March, 1820, he was called as pastor, in which office he continued until his death, Feb. 23d, 1821. From this time until May, 1823, the church was without a pastor. They had occasional preaching by Elders Robert Elliott, Tyra Harris and Royce McCoy. In Nov., 1822, Elijah Veach, a member of the church, was licensed to preach, and occasionally preached for them. In May, 1823, Elder Samuel Anderson was called to the pastorate of the church, and continued pastor until December, 1827. In July, 1825, John Graham, then a member of the church, was ordained a minister of the Gospel. In August, the same year, a Sunday-school was organized, being the first Sunday-school orgonized by the church, and one among the first organized in this Western country.

In Sept., 1823, Wm. Polke and wife joined Isaac McCoy as missionaries among the Indians, where he remained about one year, and then returned to Maria Creek. In Dec., 1826, Elder Samuel Anderson accepted, with the consent of the church, an appointment from a missionary society in Massachusetts, to travel and preach as a missionary for six months, between the Wabash and White rivers. During these years, from 1820 to Dec. 1827, the church continued to prosper, having received during that time, by letter 8, and by baptism 40 members. In addition to the preaching by the pastor Elder Anderson, and Elder Abner Davis, frequently preached within the bounds of the church, in the years 1826 and 1827.

Oct., 1827, the following record appears on the church records:

"Bro. Thomas Kennedy handed in a letter from Lamotte church, stating their happiness at the reconciliation that was effected at the last Union Association by the messengers of the two churches, and expressing a wish to cultivate Christian union and friendship.

"On motion, the church unanimously say they are equally happy, and reciprocate the same friendly feeling."

This record requires some explanation. In 1826 Lamotte Church split on the doctrine of the two seeds, as put forth and advocated by Daniel Parker. One part of the church following Parker in his advocacy of that doctrine; the other part following Thos. Kennedy, denying the doctrine. Both parties claimed to be Lamotte Church. The Wabash Association recognized Parker and his party as properly Lamotte Church, to the exclusion of Kennedy and his party. The latter then sought admission into Union Association, and upon the reconciliation with Maria Creek Church above noted, were admitted."

Elder Samuel Anderson's pastorate ceased at the end of the year 1827. In May, 1828, Elder Abner Davis was called to the pastorate of the church.

In May, 1829, Wm. Polke, church clerk, moved to Vincennes. He had served the church as clerk from its organization, in May, 1809, until May, 1829, with the exception of a little over one year, while he was away as a missionary to the Indians, a period of twenty years. Upon his removal to Vincennes, James Polke was elected clerk.

June 20th, 1829, the following record appears:

"The church agrees to take into consideration at her next meeting the consistency or inconsistency of having written Articles of Faith, other than the Scriptures."

"July 17th, 1829. The reference from last meeting respecting the consistency or inconsistency of having written Articles of Faith, taken up. On motion of Bro. Wm. Bruce the matter be laid over until next meeting, which motion was overruled.

"On motion of Bro. Samuel Chambers, that we consider the matter referred from last meeting. Which motion carried.

"After considerable discussion the following was unanimously agreed to, viz: That the believing or not believing in the utility of written Articles of Faith, should be no bar to fellowship."

This was the first action of the church upon a subject that finally resulted in the division of the church. This, however, was not the beginning of the agitation upon that subject. As early as 1823 Alexander Campbell commenced the agitation of the subject in a monthly periodical published by himself, called the Christian Baptist, and had constantly and violently opposed creeds and confessions of faith; and many people all over the country had been carried away by his teachings, among these quite a number of the members of Maria Creek Church.

The opposition to creeds was not apparently based upon

any charge of false doctrine contained in them; but upon any and all written or formal declarations of doctrine whether true or false. He, Campbell, says, that in his opposition to creeds, he differs from all others. "Our opposition" he says, "to creeds arose from a conviction that whether the opinions in them were true or false, they were hostile to the union, peace, harmony, purity and joy of Christians, and adverse to the conversion of the world to Christ," Chris. Sys. P. 9.

The above extracts from the records of the church show that this, or something of this kind, was their idea. The question was not to consider the doctrines, but the *utility* of having a written creed; and the action of the church appears to be an attempt to quiet the agitation by declaring that "believing or not believing in the *utility* of written Articles of Faith should be no bar to fellowship."

After the above action of the church, she appears to have moved along quietly and prosperously, under the ministerial labors of Elder Abner Davis, until April, 1830 and afterwards under Elder Alexander Evans, until Feb. 1832. From Jan., 1828 to Feb., 1832, she had received by letter fifteen and by baptism seventy-two members. The whole number of persons baptized into Maria Creek Church from its organization until Feb., 1832, was one hundred and ninety-six (196) and received by letter and relation seventy-one (71.) Total received into the church 267. Her membership at this time, 1832, was one hundred and seventy-one, (171).' But now the following record appears:

"Feb. 18th, 1832. An application of Wm. Bruce and others for letters of dismission in order to be constituted in a church at Bruceville.

BRUCEVILLE, Feb. 17th, 1832.

DEAR BRETHREN: Hoping that it would be for the honor of our Divine Master, and our own convenience and comfort, we request of you, (if you think us worthy,) letters of dismission, in order that we may be constituted a Church of Christ at Bruceville; and as we are so circumstanced that it is not convenient for us to attend, we have sent this our request by our beloved Brethren, David Lemen and Andrew Burnsides, to the church at Maria Creek. Wm. Bruce, David Lemen, Andrew Burnsides, Obed Macy. Jane Burnsides, Lucinda Macy, Nancy Howard and Rebecca Simpson."

"The church, after consultation on the request, agrees to dismiss the Brethren for the purpose of constituting themselves into a church of Jesus Christ in the manner that to them seems most agreeable to the laws of Jesus Christ as set forth in the New Testament. And such other Brethren as may desire to be constituted with them are permitted to join in said constitution. As it is known that a different opinion exists among us as to what is the most proper form of a church constitution; and as the church wishes and desires the happiness of her members, the peace and prosperity of Zion in general. She hopes and believes that to dismiss all orderly, pious members as may choose to join in said constitution will tend to peace and harmony.

By order of the Church,   JOSEPH CHAMBERS, Mod.

March 17, 1832. The following letter was received from the church at Bruceville.

"The Church of Christ at Bruceville to her sister church at Maria Creek, Greeting:

Whereas, it appeared from the letter of dismission that was received by those that made application, that liberty was given to any of your members that wished to unite with us in a constitution to do so; and accordingly the following persons came forward and had their names enrolled, to-wit: William Polke, Sally Polke, Nancy Polke, Jesse Hollingsworth, Betsy Lindsey, Sally Threldkill, Robert Lemen, Jane Lemen, Rhoda Morris, Nancy Ruby, Michael Crooks, Samuel D. Piety and Eliza Piety. By order of the church, March 11th 1832.

                      WILLIAM BRUCE, Acting Clk.

This organization at Bruceville was constituted, as they declared, upon the Bible alone. They made no declaration of doctrines or written Articles of Faith, to distinguish themselves from any other denomination whatever either Protestant or Catholic; or as to their understanding of what the Bible taught upon any of the leading doctrines of the Gospel.

They very soon, however, began to declare from their

Pulpit what *they understood* the Bible to teach, and to condemn all who did not agree with them.

When they attacked, not only the propriety of written Articles of Faith, but the doctrines and principles set forth in the Articles of Faith of Maria Creek Church, she felt that some action of the church was necessary in regard to her relations with the Bruceville organization. Accordingly at the July meeting following the organization at Bruceville, "Bro. Samuel Chambers brought forward for the consideration of the Church, the relation in which the Bruceville Church stands to Maria Creek Church; and whether, under existing circumstances, we invite them to seats and communion with Maria Creek Church. After some conversation the Church agrees to refer the matter to her next meeting."

"The Church directs the Clerk to draw off the Articles of Faith and rules of decorum on our Church Book."

"August 18th, 1832. The reference from our last meeting respecting the relationship in which the Bruceville Church stands toward Maria Creek Chuch, called for and read to the church. After reading a letter from Bro. William Polke, a member of the Bruceville Church, the Bruceville members present invited to seats, and have the privilege of speaking on the subject to be discussed in regard to their relations to Maria Creek Church.

"After spending several hours of investigation on the above reference, on motion of Bro. Samuel Chambers the following decision was concurred in by a majority of the church. The church are of opinion that under all the circumstances attendant therein, as some of her members have conscientious scruples on the subject, that it would be improper at present to invite the members of the Bruceville Church to our Councils or Communion Table. We hope that the members of both churches will endeavor to conduct themselves in a way that will be most likely to bring about a more happy state of things."

This hope was not to be realized. The professed reason for the division of the church was a difference of opinion as to the *utility* of written articles of faith. But it soon became apparent that there was a wide difference of opinion as to doctrine. The party that went off from the church very soon attacked, not only the utility or propriety of written articles of faith, but the doctrines contained in them, and began to promulgate and teach doctrines and principles widely at variance with those professed and taught by Baptist churches. The Baptists defended their doctrines, and very often retaliated by attacking and condemning the doctrines of the Reformers, as they at that time called themselves. So that, instead of conducting themselves in a way to bring about a better state of things, the breach widened. Bitterness came up between them, and all hope of any reconciliation was destroyed. The Reformers made every effort possible to proselyte from the Baptist churches. The writer well remembers hearing one of their prominent preachers say from the pulpit more than once, that they were especially glad to receive members coming from the Baptist church.

They were for awhile successful in proselyting from Maria CreekC hurch. It appeared at one time as if they would almost entirely absorb the whole church. During the two years and six months after the organization at Bruceville, at which time twenty-six members went out, the records show that thirty-six additional members had left Maria Creek Church to join that organization. It is probable that there were others, not mentioned in the records, that had left to join that, or some other like organization. In Feb., 1833, a number of the members living on Shaker prairie, requested and obtained letters, for the purpose of organizing a church. This whole church, after its organization, went over to the Reformers.

In August, 1835, two years and six months after the organization at Bruceville, there remained in Maria Creek Church, eighty-six members.

In Feb., 1834, the following record appears on her church book:

"On motion of Brother Joseph Chambers, the church agreed to reconsider the vote of the church passed on the Third Saturday in July, 1829, to-wit: That the believing or not believing in the utility of written Articles of Faith should be no bar to fellowship (see page 70). When, on motion of Bro. William Hargis, agreed to strike out this supplement (so called) to our Articles of Faith simply with a view to restore the Articles of Faith of this church to their proper place and influence as at our first constitution."

It is to be said of Maria Creek Church, that in all this unhappy dissention and division, she was never the aggressor. At the commencement of the trouble she exhibited a liberal and Christian spirit towards the discontented members, in declaring, although she was constituted on written Articles of Faith, that the belief or disbelief in their *utility*, should be no bar to fellowship; and when they finally determined to leave the church and form a separate organization, gave them letters and dismissed them in all Christian kindness; and this too, when it was altogether probable they knew that those they were thus kindly dismissing, would in the end prove to be enemies that would turn against them, and seek the utter destruction of Maria Creek Church. During these troubles and while the rapid defection of members was going on, some of the members that remained, became very much discouraged. The writer of these lines has heard some of them say they felt sometimes like giving up. But converted men and women, filled with the Spirit of Christ, could not give up. The love of the truth constrained them to continue the struggle, and besides this, there were too many tender memories clustering around the old church. In it they had toiled and labored for the Master. In it they had rejoiced and been made happy by exhibitions of God's love and mercy. In it they had prayed and wept together. The old church was too dear to them to be abandoned to its enemies. And so they labored on, and by the blessing of God maintained the organization of the church, with all its principles unimpaired, to be a home and a blessing for their children and children's children.

It is to be further said of these controversies; viz: The missionary controversy, and the controversy about creeds, that a false issue was presented by the party opposed to missions, and by the party opposed to creeds. The antimission spirit of the one, and unbelief in the doctrines of the Articles of Faith of the other, were at the bottom of these controversies; as the subsequent history of these parties abundantly prove. The talk about the *methods* of the missionaries, and the *utility* of creeds, were but pretexts, that in some measure obscured for the time, the real grounds of difference. But let it be remembered to the honor of Maria Creek Church, that throughout these contentions and trials she remained steadfast and true to the principles and spirit of missions, and to the doctrines of the Gospel as set forth in her Articles of Faith. "And the rain decended, and the floods came, and the winds blew, and beat upon that house, and it fell not, for it was founded upon a rock."

CHAPTER VI.

The pastorate of Alexander Evans terminated in May, 1832. From this time until April, 1834, the church was without a pastor. They had occasional preaching by Elders Brice Fields and M. Fairfield.

In Oct., 1833, the church agreed to hold a meeting once per month at Edwardsport, and from that time until April, 1843, the church met for business twice in each month alternately at Maria Creek and Edwardsport.

Elder William Stansel was called to the pastorate of the church in May, 1834, and continued in that office until 1839. He received into the fellowship of the church during this time fifty members.

The church house on Maria Creek was no longer centrally located, nearly all the members living east of it, and in Nov., 1835, the Church changed their place of meeting to a school house near Joseph Chambers'.

From 1839 to April, 1841, the Church was again without a pastor, but had occasional preaching by Elders Wm. Stansel, A. Stark, M. Betts, and John Graham.

At the last mentioned date, Elder Stansel was again employed by the Church one-fourth of his time at Edwardsport. In April, 1841, sixteen members of the Church were dismissed for the purpose of organizing Indian Creek Church.

In June, 1841, a movement was made to build a house at Edwardsport. A lot was purchased and a house partly erected; but from various causes was never completed, and the property was afterwards sold. The old brick church on Maria Creek was fast going to decay, and at the time the movement was made to build at Edwardsport, measures were taken to save, in some way, the old house. These measures resulted in its removal to the present location of Maria Creek Church. It was said by some of the Reformers that the Baptists did not act right in this matter; that they had contributed to the building of the old house, and that the Baptists ought to pay them something. In reference to this the following record will be of interest, and show the facts in the case:

"August 13, 1842. The following motion made by Alexander Chambers, that Joseph Chambers, Joseph Willis and John Keith are hereby requested and directed to attend to the property on Maria Creek; to make sale, rebuild or repair, as the interests of the church may require, after consulting the interests of all parties connected therewith, and endeavor to save the house, to the satisfaction of all who may feel an interest in the same, and report their proceedings monthly to the church."

"April, 1843. The committee appointed to attend to the old meeting house report as follows, to-wit: The undersigned committee appointed to take charge of the old meeting house and sell it if a fair price could be had for it, would now report, that James Polke, on the part of the Reform Church, proffers to give seventy-five dollars in trade on or before next Christmas; or they will take fifty dollars in the same kind of pay.

JOSEPH CHAMBERS, for Com."

"After hearing the above report the church say that she is not willing to accede to either of the above offers."

"June 17th, 1843. Whereas we have been this day informed that some of the members of the reform church attended our last meeting for the purpose of making some further propositions concerning the Brick Meeting House. On motion the church appointed Brethren Joseph Chambers, John Keith and David Chambers, a committee, who are authorized to transact any and all business that may be necessary with the said reform church, concerning the property of Maria Creek Church vested in the old Brick Meeting House; and to enter into writings with them, and as far as possible bring the whole subject to a close upon fair and honorable principles, as near as can be done."

"July, 1843. The committee appointed to make some arrangements with the reform church about the old meeting house, report as follows, to-wit: We the undersigned committee, appointed by Maria Creek Church to make offers of the Old Brick Meeting House to the Reform brethren in the vicinity of said house, as some acted liberally in building the same. The following are the terms on which we propose to let the said reform church have our right and title to the ground and all the property attached to said meeting house. We will submit the valuation of the property to disinterested men, and take one-half of the value thereof in materials, such as lumber and shingles, at the market price, delivered at such place as may be directed by the building committee of Maria Creek Church, for the purpose of erecting a new house, but under no circumstances will we agree to pay anything for the old house, and then move and rebuild the same.

Joseph Chambers,
John Keith, } Committee."
David Chambers,

This proposition was not accepted; so it appears that both parties thought it was all the old house was worth to either move it and rebuild, or to repair it where it stood; accordingly Maria Creek Church, holding the legal title to the property, proceeded to take the old house down and rebuild it on the lot now occupied by a new church, erected in 1859.

During the year 1842 Elder Herring visited and preached occasionally for the church. In August of this year the Church was very much gratified by a visit of her first pastor, Elder Isaac McCoy, who was, at this time, laboring as a missionary among the Indians west of the Missouri river. He was bent with age and feeble in body, ready to be called home, and could say, with Paul, "He had fought a good fight and kept the faith."

Soon after the expiration of Elder Stansel's year at Edwardsport, in April, 1842, the church discontinued her regular meetings at that place, but continued to hold occasional meetings there, as quite a number of her members resided in that vicinity.

In Jan., 1843, Elder Murdock McRae was invited to preach at the regular monthly meetings at Maria Creek, and in Jan., 1844, was called and accepted the pastoral care of the church; which office he continued to fill, to the general satisfaction of the church, until Feb., 1851. During his pastorate the church was reasonably prosperous, having received into its fellowship one hundred and nine members. There were some difficulties came up in the church that, for awhile, seriously threatened its peace

HISTORY OF MARIA CREEK CHURCH. 83

and harmony, but by careful management and the exercise of a Christian spirit by the parties concerned, they were amicably settled.

Elder McRae had the assistance, during his pastorate, of occasional preaching by Elders Wm. Stansel, John Graham, Daniel Stark, and B. B. Arnold. Under the preaching of Elders McRae and Arnold, a number of members living about eight miles north-east of Maria Creek, where there had once been a Baptist church, called Shiloh, were received into Maria Creek Church. In March, 1851, sixteen of these members were dismissed, who organized Bethel Church.

At the termination of Elder McRae's pastorate, Elder Stansel was preaching as a missionary in Union Association, and preached occasionally for the church, until Jan., 1853, at which time he again took the pastoral charge of the church, and continued to serve the church as pastor, until March, 1855, being occasionally assisted by Elders McRae, Robb and Elkana Allen.

Elder J. L. Irwin was next called to the pastorate and preached for the church until April, 1856, at which time he removed to Minnesota. The year following, the church had occasional preaching by Elders James Hooper, McRae, Robb and Stansel. In June, 1857, Elder J. L. Irwin returned, and again became pastor of the church, which office he continued to fill until August, 1860.

In Nov., 1858, the church was called to mourn the death of Deacon Joseph Chambers. Bro. Chambers had united with Maria Creek Church Jan., 1811, and for forty-seven years lived a devoted Christian life in the church; always working for her interest, and for the building up and the extension of Christ's Kingdom. He had filled acceptably to the church the offices of Deacon, Moderator and Clerk. He was an industrious, honest, earnest, pious, devoted Christian man, and by his labors, his counsels and his example did more for Maria Creek Church than any other one member since her organization, and had the inexpressable happiness of seeing his whole family of eleven children baptized into the church.

In June, 1858, eighteen members were dismissed to go into the organization of a church at Edwardsport.

A large and substantial brick church-house was erected in the year 1859 at Maria Creek.

The period from 1850 to 1860 was peaceful and prosperous for the church. She received into her fellowship during that time one hundred and twenty-seven members. Among them I find the name of T. J. Keith, who joined the church in March, 1856, when quite young. During the war of 1861-5 he served his country as a soldier. Upon his return home he went to Shurtleff College, at Upper Alton, Ills., where he was graduated in the Theological department of that institution, immediately after which he entered the ministry; and in 1871 he, with his wife, was sent by the Baptist Board of Foreign Missions to India, where he remained four years and nine months, until his health became impaired, when he returned to the United States, and at the present time is pastor of the Baptist Church at Vincennes, Indiana.

In Nov., 1860, Elder Robert Moore was called to the pastorate of the Church.

The excitement upon the political questions, the secession movement, and the war that followed, and which more or less seriously affected the churches all over the land, had its effect on Maria Creek Church as on other churches. Her members were almost, if not quite all, in sympathy with the Government in its prosecution of the war. They were, in the language of the time, Unionists. And when two members from another Baptist Church, who had been excluded in consequence of difficulties growing out of the political questions of the time, presented themselves for membership, under the excitement of the time, and moved by their sympathies for these excluded brethren, and believing it was right under the circumstances that existed at that time, she received them into her fellowship. At her next meeting nine more members from the same church presented themselves, not having been excluded, but without letters of dismission, they also were received.

All these were received without consulting the church from which they came.

This action of Maria Creek Church cannot be justified according to Baptist usage, nor Christian courtesy. It can only be excused, and that on account of the excitement of the time. This, it is supposed, the church from which these members came did; as they never made any complaint. After the war was over and the excitement had subsided, Maria Creek Church passed the following resolution:

"Resolved, that the action of the Church heretofore in receiving excluded members from sister churches, shall not be made a precedent governing the future action of the Church in like cases."

April, 1864. Warren C. Keith was granted a license to preach; and in Feb., 1866, was ordained by Maria Creek Church to the work of the ministry. Brother Keith had joined Maria Creek Church by baptism in 1852. Immediately after his ordination he took the pastoral care of Indian Creek Church. This church dissolved in 1870 and reorganized at Bicknell, on the I. & V. R. R. Elder Keith continued as pastor of the Church after its reorganization. He also preached for various Churches in Union Association up to the time of his death, which occurred April the 28th, 1874, aged 55 years.

Elder Keith was a devoted, pious man and a good preacher; and although he had no educational advantages in early life, he was a close thinker, a careful student of the Bible and a great reader. Consequently he accumulated a large amount of biblical and useful knowledge and a good stock of sound theology. His funeral was preached by Elder F. Slater, from Revelations xiv chap. and 13th verse, "And I heard a voice saying unto me, Write, blessed are the dead that die in the Lord from henceforth; yea, saith the Spirit, that they may rest from their labors; and their works do follow them."

Elder Moore was continued as pastor of the church until Sept., 1867. During his pastorate, sixty-three members were added to the church. His ministry was very acceptable to the church and at the time of his resignation, (Sept., 1867,) the following resolutions were passed by the church:

"*Resolved*, That in parting with Brother Moore, who has been our efficient pastor for nearly seven years, in building up the church, and in the ingathering of precious souls, we sustain a loss not easily filled.

2d. We hereby recommend him to those with whom his lot may be cast, as a faithful minister of the Gospel of Christ.

3d. That these resolutions be recorded on the church book, and a copy be given to Brother Moore, and a copy sent to the Christian Times and Witness for publication."

From Sept., 1867, to Dec., 1867, the church was again without a pastor. At the later date Elder Wm. Stansel was, for the fourth time, called to the pastorate of the church. He was continued as pastor until Sept., 1869. Elder Wm. Stansel was pastor of Maria Creek Church in all ten years. He also preached frequently for the church in the times intervening between his pastorates.

Elder Stansel was a man greatly beloved by Maria Creek Church. His preaching was always acceptable to them; a man of fine social qualities, beloved by all, but especially by the young people, over whom he always wielded a strong influence for good, and withal an earnest, faithful minister of the Gospel of Christ.

From Sept., 1869, the church had no pastor, until March, 1870, at which time Elder J. L. Irwin was again called to the pastorate; and served the church as pastor and moderator until Nov., 1872. During this period the church moved along quietly, and thirty-one members were received into the fellowship of the church. Elder Irwin was three times pastor of the church, and served the church altogether in that office seven years and two months. He was much esteemed as a man and as a minister by the church, and by all with whom he came in contact. He was a faithful minister of the Gospel.

The church was again without a pastor until March, 1873, when Elder F. Slater took pastoral charge of the church for one year, at the expiration of which time Elder G. W. Melten was called to the pastorate, and preached for the church until Dec., 1874.

Jan., 1875, Elder A. C. Edwards was called, and for two years served the church, preaching both at the church and at Freelandville, two miles north-east of the church.

During Bro. Edwards' pastorate twenty members were added to the Church.

At the expiration of Brother Edwards' time (Jan., 1877) Elder R. A. Taylor was called and accepted the pastorate. He preached for the church until the following August, in which time six members were added to the church.

For some cause unknown to the church Elder Taylor abandoned the pastorate, leaving the church without a pastor until April, 1878, when Elder A. B. Robertson was called to the pastorate, and preached for the church until Dec., 1878.

Feb., 1879, Elder J. W. Hammack was called to the pastorate and served the church until Dec., 1881. During his pastorate thirty-four members were added to the church. At the termination of Elder Hammack's pastorate, the church employed Elijah Sanford, a licentiate of the Edwardsport Baptist Church, to preach for them one-half of his time as a supply, and in April, 1882, Elder C. B. Allen was called to the pastorate and preached to church in conjunction with Brother Sanford, until Dec., 1882.

In Feb., 1883, Elder Sanford, having in the mean time been ordained, took pastoral charge of the church and remains until the present time, (Jan. 1st, 1889,) their efficient and beloved pastor.

Since Elder Sanford commenced preaching for the church in Jan., 1882, she has received into her fellowship sixty-eight members.

For the last fifty-four years, (since 1835,) the church has moved along quietly and peacefully. No serious disturbance has occurred to mar her peace or disturb her harmony.

Maria Creek Church has now been in existence almost four score years, and has been a continual illustration of the words of Christ to His disciples: "Ye are the light of the world," "Ye are the salt of the earth." She has always been true to the principles upon which she was constituted, and to the doctrines of the Gospel as she understood them. She has remained true to the missionary cause for which she contended so earnestly in the earlier years of her history, and has ever contributed according to her ability to all the missionary enterprises carried on by the Baptists of the United States, of the State, and of the association to which she belongs.

During all the years of her existence, she has kept up her regular stated meetings, administered the ordinances of the church, maintained her discipline, and by her example and through her ministry has held forth the doctrines of the Gospel of Christ to all within her borders, and has been a power for good in the world; as all will testify, who are acquainted with her history.

All the old members who took part in her organization, and shared in her struggles and controversies about missions and articles of faith, have gone to their reward. The church they established remains to cherish their memory and carry on the work they began. Another generation now occupies her pews and pulpit. They do not carry, as their fathers did, their rifles and muskets with them to church; nor post a sentinel to guard them against Indian surprises while they worship.

The forests that once surrounded their place of meeting have all disappeared, and fields of grain, blue-grass pastures and apple orchards have taken their places. The screaming wild-cat, nor the howling wolf are no longer heard, but instead the crowing cock, the bleating lambs, and lowing kine. In the beautiful grove surrounding their meeting house, grown from the acorn long since their church was organized, children play and gather wild flowers to decorate the pulpit, or present to their Sunday-School teachers. In this quiet country church, away from the noise and confusion of town or city, the people meet and worship in peace the God of their Fathers.

"The wilderness and the solitary place shall be glad for them, and the desert shall blossom as the rose. It shall blossom abundantly, and rejoice, even with joy and singing; the glory of Lebanon shall be given unto it, the excellencey of Carmel and Sharon; they shall see the glory of the Lord and the excellency of our God. Strengthen ye the weak hands, and confirm the feeble knees. Say to them that are of a fearful heart: Be strong, fear not; behold your God will come with vengeance, even God with a recompense; He will come and save you. Then the eyes of the blind shall be opened, and the ears of the deaf shall be unstopped. Then shall the lame man leap as a hart, and the tongue of the dumb sing: For in the wilderness shall waters break out, and streams in the desert. And the parched ground shall become a pool, and the thirsty land springs of water. In the habitation of dragons, where each lay, shall be grass with reeds and rushes. And a highway shall be there, and a way, and it shall be called the way of holiness; the unclean shall not pass over it; but it shall be for those; the wayfaring men, though fools, shall not err therein. No lion shall be there, nor any ravenous beast shall go up thereon, it shall not be found there; but the redeemed shall walk there and the ransomed of the Lord shall return and come to Zion with songs and everlasting joy upon their heads; they shall obtain joy and gladness, and sorrow and sighing shall flee away."

———o———

MINISTERS.

Names of Ministers who have served Maria Creek Church as Pastors, and the date and time of service:
Isaac McCoy, from January, 1810, to October, 1818.
Aaron Frakes, from March, 1820, to February, 1821.
Samuel Anderson, from May, 1823, to December, 1827.
Abner Davis, from May, 1828, to April, 1830.
Alexander Evans, from May, 1830, to February, 1832.
William Stansel. from May, 1834, to December, 1838.
" " from May, 1841, to April, 1842.
Murdoc McRae, from January, 1844, to February, 1851.
William Stansel, from January, 1853, to March, 1855.
J. L. Irwin, from April, 1855, to April, 1856.
" " from June, 1857, to August, 1860.
Robert Moore, from November, 1860, to September, 1867.
William Stansel, from December, 1867, to September, 1869.
J. L. Irwin, from March, 1870, to November, 1872.
E. Slater, from March, 1873, to March, 1874.
G. W. Melton, from April, 1874, to December, 1874.
A. C. Edwards, from January, 1875 to December, 1876.
R. A. Taylor, from January, 1877, to August, 1877.
A. B. Robertson, from April, 1878, to February, 1879:
J. W. Hammack, from April, 1879, to December, 1881.
C. B. Allen, from April, 1882, to December, 1882.
Elijah Sanford, from February, 1883, to present time.

MEMBERS.

Names of all the members found upon the records of Maria Creek Church, who have been received into her fellowship from her organization until the present time, Jan. 1st, 1889, and the date of their admission so far as it could be ascertained:

CHARTER MEMBERS.

Samuel Allison,
Phoebe Allison,
Charles Polke, Sr.,
Charles Polke, Jr.,
Margaret Polke,
Achsah Polke,

William Polke,
Sally Polke,
John Lemen,
Polly Lemen,
William Bruce,
Sally Bruce.

John Morris, (colored).

Name	Month	Day, Year
Richard Carson	November	—, 1809
Susanna McCord	"	—, "
Isaac McCoy	January,	—, 1810
Christiana McCoy	"	—, "
Thos. Kennedy	June	16, "
Elizabeth Kennedy	"	" "
Elizabeth Brown	July	17, "
Joseph Liston	October	17, "
Nancy Liston	"	" "
Joseph Chambers	January	19, 1811
Elizabeth Chambers	"	" "
William McCord	"	" "
Polly Chambers	"	" "
Delilah Liston	June	15, "
Elizabeth Moore	"	" "
William Drake	July	20, "
Sally Drake	February	15, 1812
Peter Hansbrough	March	14, 1812
Elizabeth Hansbrough	"	" "
Polly Hansbrough	"	" "

Nancy Hansbrough.............	"	" "
Thomas Mills	"	" "
Lydia Mills.......................	"	" "
Polly Thomas	May	16, "
Emmet Thomas..................	July	16, 1814
Nancy Ruby.......................	August	20, "
Thomas Piety.....................	November	26, "
Polly Piety.........................	"	" "
Elizabeth Piety...................		
Betsy Paget.......................	June	17, 1815
Jonathan Cox.....................	October	14, "
George (colored man).........	January	20, 1816
Ephraim West....................	"	21, "
Lewis Noel........................	June	15, "
Sarah Noel........................	"	" "
Phoebe Allison..................	"	" "
John Mills	"	22, "
Richard Highsmith.............	"	" "
Richard Allison.................	"	" "
Martha Hunt.....................	"	" "
Eleanor Lemaster..............	"	" "
John Allison.....................	"	" "
Daniel Allison..................	July	21, "
Sally Highsmith	"	" "
Mathew Stewart...............	"	" "
Lucy Barnet	"	26, "
Polly Free.......................	"	" "
Caleb Kemp.....................	August	9 "
Susanna Murphy...............	October	19, "
Elizabeth Kester...............	"	" "
Joseph Thompson.............	May	17, 1817
Nancy Thompson.............	"	" "
Hannah Willis..................	September	2, "

HISTORY OF MARIA CREEK CHURCH. 95

Rebecca Chambers...	June	13, 1818
William Keith	December	15, "
Elizabeth Keith	"	" "
Richard Brock	January	19, 1819
Robert Lemen	April	18, "
Susanna Polke	"	" "
Elizabeth Polke	"	" "
John Lemen	"	" "
Henry Ransford	May	7, "
Sally McKee	"	" "
Samuel Lemen	"	16, "
Robert Piety	"	" "
Thos. Piety, Jr.,	"	" "
Delilah Ruby	"	" "
Polly Lemen, Jr	"	" "
Cynthia Polke	"	" "
Jane Lemen	"	" "
James Chambers	"	" "
Wm. D. Bruce	"	" "
Anna Lindsay	"	" "
Sally Duty	"	" "
Margaret Piety	"	" "
Levi Chambers	"	" "
Katharine Carico	"	" "
Sally Duty, Sr.	June	19, 1819
John Chambers	"	" "
Samuel Medley	"	" "
Delilah Hansbrough	"	" "
Jesse Hollingsworth	"	20, "
James Medley	"	" "
Nancy Chambers	"	" "
John Hollingsworth	July	17, "
Nelly Hollingsworth	"	" "

7

Jesse (colored man)	July	17,	1819
Jesse Haddan	"	"	"
Samuel Lindsay	"	"	"
Robert Polke	"	"	"
Polly Hollingsworth	"	18,	"
Lydia Chambers	"	"	"
David Lemen	"	"	"
Lucy Medley	"	"	"
Spear S. Bruce	August	14,	"
George Lindsay	September	20,	"
John Medley	"	"	"
Polly Hulen	"	"	"
Peter Caress	October	16,	"
Nancy Medley	"	18,	"
Milly Hulen	"	28,	"
Lydia Perdue	"	"	"
Rebecca Hulen	"	"	"
Micajah Bicknell	November	20,	"
Ambrose Hulen	"	"	"
John Bicknell	"	22,	"
Samuel Gardner	"	"	"
Betsy Duty	"	"	"
Betsy Bicknell	"	"	"
Polly Bicknell	February	19,	1820
Patsy Goodman	”	”	”
Samuel Chambers	”	”	”
Jacob Booker	March	18,	”
John Hansbrough	”	”	”
Robert Smith	April	26,	”
Patsey Medley	May	20,	”
Betsy Miller	”	”	”
Nancy Piety	”	”	”
Nancy Morris	”	”	”

Wm. Morris............................	May	21, 1820
Wm. Mathes............................	June	17, "
Bartley Goodman.....................	"	" "
Wm. Knight............................	"	18, "
Alfred Bicknell......................	September	17, "
Margaret Hart........................	November	18, "
Elijah Veach..........................	April	21, 1822
Jemima Lykins.......................	November	16, "
Edward H. Piper.....................	July	19, 1823
Zacariah Poore.......................	August	16, "
George McCord......................	December	21, "
Eleanor Piety.........................	March	20, 1824
Sarah Clark...........................	April	17, "
David McGraw.......................	"	" "
Martha Emery........................	"	18, "
Toby Emery...........................	May	15, "
Samuel Anderson...................	July	16, "
Elizabeth Roller.....................	"	19, "
Polly Hill...............................	June	18, 1825
Benjamin Ochiltree.................	August	19, "
Maria Roller..........................	"	" "
Jane Johnson.........................	"	" "
Rodolphus Lamb....................	"	20, "
David Chambers.....................	October	15, "
Mumford Bicknell..................	"	" "
James Ashby.........................	"	" "
Polly Hulen...........................	"	" "
Lucy Hatcher.........................	"	27, "
Edward Hatcher.....................	"	" "
Matilda Hulen.......................	"	" "
Nancy Hulen.........................	"	" "
Wyatt Hulen.........................	November	19, "
Eleazor Godfrey....................	"	25, "

Jane Ashby	November	25, 1825
Jane Hulen	"	" "
Nancy Bicknell	January	14, 1826
Sarah Frances	April	15, "
Daniel Blessing	"	" "
John Embry	May	20, "
Charles Polke, Jr.	June	17, "
Jacob Wolf	"	" "
Lucas Dedrick	July	29, "
Elizabeth Hulen	"	" "
Mary Simonson	"	" "
Caesar Embry	February	17, 1827
Delilah Jarrell	August	17, "
Wm. Hulen	September	30, "
Polly Hopkins	"	" "
Sally Buckles	"	" "
Jonathan P. Cox	October	20, "
Wm. Comstock	"	" "
Nancy Polke (daughter of Wm. P.	"	" "
Sally Chambers	"	" "
Nancy Polke (daughter of Ch. P.)	November	17, "
Rachel Bruce	May	17, 1828
Jane Ganoe	June	14, "
Patsy Ganoe	Not Recorded.	
Nancy Shepard	June	15, "
Nancy Keith (daughter of Wm. K.)	"	" "
John H. McKee	July	19, "
Huldah Piety	"	" "
Joseph Wolf	"	20, "
Rebecca Wolf	"	21, "
John Wolf	"	" "
Mary Wolf	"	" "
Polly Boyd	August	2, "

HISTORY OF MARIA CREEK CHURCH. 99

Vance Wolf....................................	August	2, 1828
Isabel Shepard...............................	"	" "
Sally Adams..................................	"	" "
Hannah Shepard............................	"	" "
Isaac Horr.....................................	"	" "
Margaret Chambers.......................	"	16, "
Polly Chambers.............................	"	" "
Amy Keith.....................................	"	" "
Bennett Mason..............................	"	" "
Barnard Hollingsworth..................	"	30, "
Rachel Cox....................................	"	" "
Thos. Hulen..................................	"	31, "
James Boyd...................................	September	2, "
Caroline Ethridge..........................	November	16, "
Samuel D. Piety............................	June	21, 1829
Eliza Piety.....................................	"	" "
Amy Biddy....................................	"	" "
Jane Bursides................................	"	" "
Lucinda Bruce...............................	"	" "
John Fitz-Patrick...........................	July	17, "
Joseph Willis.................................	"	18, "
Priscilla Davis...............................	August	15, "
Barns Reeves.................................	"	16, "
Absalom Hill.................................	"	24, "
Wm. Vantrest................................	"	30, "
Jacob Crooks and wife..................	September	13, "
Lewis Reeves.................................	"	" "
Michael Crooks.............................	"	18, "
Charles Jarrell and wife................	"	" "
Polly Boyd....................................	May	9, 1830
Mary Ann Bailey...........................	"	" "
Sally Thrailkill..............................	July	18, "
Harrison Hustead..........................	October	28, "

Mrs. Joseph Willis	November	21,	1830
Lucinda Macy	March	19,	1831
Anna Piety	"	"	"
Permelia Bicknell	May	19,	"
Henry Bailey	"	"	"
Elizabeth Polke	"	20,	"
Charles Polke, Jr	"	"	"
Nancy Cox	"	"	"
Nancy Howard	June	18,	"
Susan Piety	"	19,	"
Samuel F. Chambers	"	"	"
James Martin	"	"	"
John Chambers, Jr	"	"	"
Warren C. Keith	"	"	"
Robert Bailey	"	"	"
Elizabeth Summers	"	"	"
Nancy Wolf	"	"	"
John Keith, Sr	July	16.	"
Spencer Ruby	"	"	"
Martha Dinwidie	"	"	"
Harriet Polke	"	"	"
Margaret Keith	"	"	"
Alexander Evans	"	"	"
Elizabeth Lindsay	"	17,	"
Isaac Chambers	"	"	"
Priscilla, (colored woman)	"	"	"
Maria Purdue	"	"	"
Clark Willis	August	20,	"
Wm. Hargis	September	10,	"
Elizabeth Hargis	"	"	"
Andrew Burnsides	"	"	"
Ambrose Azbell	"	"	"
Sarah Azbell	"	"	"

Nancy J. Willis	October	15,	1831
Rebecca Simpson	November	4,	"
Rhoda Morris	"	"	"
Obed Macy	December	17,	"
Mary Bowers	April	14,	1832
Michael Robertson	"	28,	"
John Cansellor	December	15,	1834
John Bicknell	"	"	"
Washington Frederick	"	"	"
Frances Frederick	"	"	"
Sally Patrick	"	"	"
Polly Godfrey	"	"	"
William Stansel	April	18,	1835
Celia Stansel	"	"	"
Lucy Green	June	13,	"
Nancy Summers	July	11,	"
Frances Hoover	"	"	"
Betsy Trammel	"	"	"
John Keith, Jr	December	18,	"
Sarah Keith	"	"	"
Elizabeth Keith	"	"	"
Henry Keith, Sr	"	"	"
Susan Keith	"	"	"
Elizabeth Jarrell	October	—,	1836
Christian Chambers	October	7,	1837
Mrs. Rucker	November	12,	"
Malinda Chambers	"	18,	"
Nancy Chambers	"	"	"
Alexander Chambers	"	"	"
Calvin Chambers	December	—,	"
Jane Jarrell	"	—,	"
Maria Jarrell	"	—,	"
Elizabeth Chambers	"	—,	"

HISTORY OF MARIA CREEK CHURCH.

Isabel Chambers	December	—, 1837
Jesse B. Keith	January	13, 1838
Wm. Ferguson	February	10, "
John L. Chambers	"	" "
Nancy Ann Chambers	March	" "
Thomas Chambers	"	11, "
Moses Robbins	"	17, "
Margaret Robbins	"	" "
Polly Ann Robertson	April	7, "
Mary Ann Turner	"	" "
Nancy Bicknell	"	?, "
John Frakes	"	" "
Nancy Frakes	"	" "
Tyra Hulen	June	9, "
Eliza Hulen	"	" "
Delilah Jarrell	"	" "
Amanda Willis	"	16, "
Rachel Chambers	"	" "
E. W. Robertson	December	8, "
Mary Hooper	February	10, 1839
Charles Hooper, Sr.	"	14. "
Nancy Goodman	November	27, 1840
Sally Ann Lawson	"	" "
Mandon Cook	December	15, "
Samuel Bicknell	"	" "
Mary Ann Godfrey	"	" "
Emily Willis	April	1, 1841
Wm. Hooper	November	13, "
Elizabeth Hooper	"	" "
Lucy Williams	"	" "
Cary Chambers	October	30, 1842
Joseph Robertson	"	" "
Charles F. Hooper	June	31, "

HISTORY OF MARIA CREEK CHURCH. 103

Susan Hooper	June	31,	1842
Polly Azbell	"	"	"
Malinda Rucker	"	"	"
Andrew T. Robertson	November	1,	"
Mary Ann Robertson	"	"	"
Elizabeth Jones	"	3	"
James Bynum	"	4,	"
Benjamin Hargis	"	"	"
Jesse Chambers	"	"	"
Samuel Chambers, Jr.	"	"	"
Malinda Johnson	"	5,	"
Aquilla Jones	"	"	"
Jane Chambers	December	21,	"
Nancy Johnson	"	"	1842
Leander Williams	January	14,	1843
James Johnson	"	28,	"
Eli Chambers	March	18,	"
Sarah Chambers	"	"	"
John Bowers	"	"	"
Emily Chambers	April	15,	"
Nancy Cox	July	16,	"
Mary J. Bicknell	August	28,	"
Lavina Chambers	"	29,	"
Jane Willis	September	22,	"
Larkin Clark	December	23,	"
Martin S. Miller	January	20,	1844
Tabner Bowen	"	21,	"
Anna Bowen	"	"	"
Nancy Keith	March	16,	"
Elizabeth Crooks	"	"	"
Geo. Smith	April	19,	"
Katharine Smith	"	"	"
Susan M. Clark	"	"	"

Elizabeth Bowers	April	19, 1844
Perry Hollingsworth	"	21, "
Sally Hollingsworth	May	18, "
Eliza Howard	November	16, "
Murdoc McRae	January	18, 1845
Sarah Ann McRae	"	" "
Mary Ann Cox	April	19, "
Elizabeth Howard	May	17, "
Wm. Jackson and wife	June	—, "
Eliza Calbertson	November	15, "
Mary Ann Keith	"	16, "
Emeline Hooper	January	18, 1846
Pinkney Hooper	"	" "
Louisa Williams	March	14, "
Thomas F. Chambers	June	20, "
Jane Chambers	"	" "
Martha Hooper	January	16, 1847
Eliza Lindsay	February	21, "
Elizabeth Miller	September	28, "
Katherine Bowers	"	" "
Solomon McArthur	August	11, 1849
Sarah McArthur	"	" "
Wm. Johnson	September	15, "
Lucinda Johnson	"	" "
Thomas McRae	"	" "
Nancy McRae	"	" "
Abraham Hollingsworth	December	16, "
B. B. Arnold	"	29, "
Anna Arnold	"	" "
Gilleland Arnold	"	" "
Srrah Hollingsworth	January	1, 1850
Elizabeth Baker	"	" "
John L. Keith	"	2, "

Margaret Bicknell	January	10,	1850
Eudemile Chambers	May	19,	"
John Hargis	"	26,	"
Andrew Carmickel	June	2,	"
Sarah Carmickel	"	"	"
Jesse Carmickel	"	"	"
Elizabeth Carmickel	"	"	"
Mary Carmickel	"	"	"
Mary Brewer	August	15,	"
Peter Carroll	"	19,	"
Mary J. Carroll	"	"	"
Marinda Delay	"	"	"
Jane Maxwell	"	28,	"
Lucinda Morris	"	"	"
Nancy Jane Delay	"	"	"
Wm. Maxwell	October	10,	"
Julia Maxwell	"	"	"
Samuel Maxwell	"	"	"
Esther Maxwell	"	"	"
Lewis Brewer	"	"	"
Mahala Miller	"	20,	"
James Maxwell	"	"	"
Anna Evans	November	16,	"
Margaret Johnson	December	30,	"
Jacob Smith	January	19,	1851
John W. Brewer	"	25,	"
Sarah Reeve	June	24,	1852
Joseph Reeve	"	"	"
Susan Hargis	August	22,	"
Joanna Carmickel	"	"	"
Joseph H. Chambers	September	5,	"
A. B. Chambers	"	"	"
Elizabeth Risley	"	"	"

Benjamin Chambers	September	6,	1852
Jane Chambers	"	"	"
Allen Sexton	"	12,	"
Sarah Sexton	"	"	"
Sarah Robbins	"	"	"
Levi Frasier	"	"	"
Sarah J. Frasier	"	"	"
Lucinda Robertson	"	"	"
Marcus Miller	"	"	"
David M. Lovelace	"	"	"
Robert Elliott	"	"	"
Mary Williams	"	"	"
Henry Keith, Jr	"	"	"
Samuel T. Chambers	"	"	"
Warren C. Keith	"	"	"
John A. Chambers	"	"	"
Fred. Sexton	"	18,	"
Polly Collins	"	"	"
Peter McCracken	October	16,	"
Nancy McCracken	"	"	"
Cam. Moore	"	"	"
Tabitha Moore	"	"	"
Emily Martin	"	"	"
Susan Fairhurst	March	20,	1853
Sarah Medley	July	16,	"
Jacob Collins	"	"	"
Mary J. Bond	February	19,	1854
Juda Sexton	March	18,	"
Austin Medley	"	19,	"
Susan Medley	"	"	"
Eliza Jones	"	"	"
Lydia Hooper	July	16,	"
David Hagar	October	4,	"

HISTORY OF MARIA CREEK CHURCH. 107

Huldah Hargis	October	4,	1854
Ruth Chambers	,,	,,	,,
Martha Williams	,,	,,	,,
Lucy Medley	,,	,,	,,
Mary Hooper	,,	,,	,,
Margaret Keith	December	16,	,,
James Cole	January	21,	1855
Minerva Cole	,,	,,	,,
Mary Keith	,,	,,	,,
David Risley	February	17,	,,
Mrs. David Risley	,,	,,	,,
Fanny Irwin	March	,,	,,
Benjamin Irwin	,,	,,	,,
Sarah Fry	August	19,	,,
Jane Cook	,,	,,	,,
Mary Smith	,,	,,	,,
Nancy Steel	,,	20,	,,
Mary Chambers	November	19,	,,
Mary Bicknell	March	17,	1856
Elizabeth Williams	,,	,,	,,
Joseph M. Robertson	,,	,,	,,
Anna Baltus	,,	19,	,,
Daniel W. Robertson	,,	,,	,,
Jane Robertson	,,	,,	,,
Elizabeth Maxwell	,,	,,	,,
James Maxwell	,,	21	,,
Harret Medley	,,	,,	,,
Henry Bicknell	,,	,,	,,
Thomas J. Keith	,,	22,	,,
Sarah Collins	,,	,,	,,
Smiley N. Chambers	,,	23,	,,
Endemile Chambers	,,	,,	,,
Martha Pace	,,	,,	,,

Katharine Crooks	March	28,	1856
Margaret Crooks	"	"	"
Charles Moore	"	"	"
Leander Chambers	"	"	"
Jane Hicks	April	17,	1858
Ben. F. Keith	"	22,	"
John Welton	"	24,	"
Henry M. Gilham	"	25,	"
Louisa Gilham	"	"	"
J. W. Chambers	"	"	"
Hiram Hooper	"	28,	"
Nancy Maxwell	"	"	"
Simeon Walker	May	2,	"
Almira Walker	"	"	"
Juda McArthur	June	19,	"
Geo. Walker	October	"	"
Eleanor Chambers	June	18,	1859
Alex. Wollerman	"	"	"
Mrs. Alex. Wollerman	"	"	"
August Miller	"	"	"
Mrs. August Miller	"	"	"
Jane Hill	October	15,	"
Mary Chambers	December	18,	"
Deborah Hunnicut	"	"	"
Frances Keith	"	"	"
Sarah J. Keith	"	"	"
Joseph Irwin	"	"	"
Geo. Irvin	January	14,	1860
Angeline Keith	"	"	"
Nancy Keith	"	"	"
Charlotte Chambers	"	"	"
Ruth Fairhurst	"	"	"
Rebecca Fairhurst	"	"	"

Sarah Chambers	January	14, 1860
Hannah Chambers	,,	,, ,,
Thos. R. Chambers	,,	,, ,,
Mary F. Robertson	,,	,, ,,
Mary A. Robertson	,,	,, ,,
Mary E. Chambers	,,	,, ,,
James Crooks	,,	,, ,,
Jonathan Crooks	,,	,, ,,
John Smith	,,	,, ,,
Margaret Keith	April	14, ,,
Peyton S. Skinner	August	17, ,,
Kinsey Watson	October	20, ,,
Elizabeth Watson	,,	,, ,,
Eliza McArthur	,,	,, ,,
Marja Risley	,,	,, ,,
Jane Risley	,,	,, ,,
Sarah McArthur	,,	,, ,,
Lucy McArthur	,,	,, ,,
Lacy Woods	January	16, 1864
Vincent Corbin	,,	,, ,,
Greenup Kimberlin	February	20, ,,
James Hinkle	,,	,, ,,
Eliza Kimberlin	,,	,, ,,
Nancy Hooper	,,	,, ,,
Lydia Corbin	,,	,, ,,
Sarah Woods	,,	,, ,,
Jane Woods	,,	,, ,,
Elizabeth Hinkle	,,	,, ,,
Mary Kimberlin	March	—, ,,
Benjamin Bowers	,,	—, ,,
O. P. Griffey	June	18, ,,
Mary J. Kutch	August	20, ,,
Nancy M. Smith	October	—, ,,

HISTORY OF MARIA CREEK CHURCH.

Mary Smith	October	—, 1864
Ann Smith	"	—, "
Lewis Robertson	Date not given	
Mary E. McClure	" "	"
Wm. Nicholson	" "	"
Daniel Robbins	" "	"
H. T. Keith	" "	"
Thomas Smith	March	19, 1865
Margaret Keith	"	" "
John Collins	"	" "
Wm. Collins	"	" "
J. N. Chambers	"	" "
Michael Chambers	"	" "
Malissa Chambers	"	" "
Hannah Collins	"	" "
Nancy L. Robertson	"	" "
Isabel Crooks	"	" "
Mary A. Robertson	"	" "
Martha Frazo	"	" "
Henry Frazo	"	" "
Harrison Hollingsworth	"	" "
A. J. Couchman	"	" "
Wm. S. Robertson	"	" "
Charles Chambers	"	" "
Geo. I. Keith	"	" "
Jas. P. Pace	"	" "
D. M. Pace	"	" "
Nancy Gilmore	"	" "
Wm. Chambers	"	" "
Lucinda Chesler	"	" "
Levi Frazo	"	" "
Mrs. Levi Frazo	"	" "
Lucy Maxwell	December 16,	"

Mary A. Bicknell	December	17, 1865
Fred. Herbzog	Date not Recorded.	
Willis Bicknell	" "	"
Herman Broksmith	May	17, 1866
Joanna Broksmith	"	" "
Jemima Begeman	April	17, 1867
Godlove Broksmith	"	" "
Helen Berry	"	" "
Sarah Wilks	June	15, "
Pettus Wilks	"	" "
Elizabeth J. Kennedy	January	17, 1869
J. N. Bennet	June	12, 1870
Rosa Keith	August	21, "
Jane Wallace	"	" "
Helen Wallace	"	" "
Eliza Walker	"	" "
N. G. Robertson	"	" "
Mary Hardesty	"	" "
John Hardesty	"	" "
Melvina Keith	"	" "
Margaret Smith	"	" "
Nancy J. Smith	"	" "
Millard F. Smith	"	" "
Therese Keith	"	" "
Wm. Elliott	February	19, 1871
Thomas F. Townsly	December	16, "
Margaret Townsly	"	" "
Delilah Townsly	"	" "
Sarah Walker	April	9, 1872
Elizabeth Wallace	"	" "
Mary Smith	"	" "
Margaret Bicknell	"	" "
Winfield Keith	"	" "

Joseph C. Robertson	April	9, 1872
Ophelia Couchman	"	" "
Margaret Chambers	"	" "
Wm. Dellinger	"	" "
Wm. T. Richardson	"	" "
Wm. Heseman	"	" "
Wm. Burnsmeier	"	" "
Eliza Richrdson	"	" "
Jas. A. Keith	"	" "
Nancy Townsly	April	20, "
Nathaniel Donham	December	15, "
Emily Donham	"	" "
Cindarilla Donham	November	16, 1873
Cynthia Donham	April	19, "
America West	June	22, "
Charles Umphries	October	18, "
Judson Walker	March	20, 1875
Sarah Cox	January	30, 1876
Alphoso Chambers	"	" "
Ada Chambers	"	" "
Alice Bicknell	"	" "
Tandy Keith	"	" "
Maron Keith	"	" "
Flora Chambers	"	" "
Ernest Bicknell	"	" "
Hattie Keith	"	" "
Jennie Chambers	"	" "
Minnie Heseman	"	" "
Matilda Crooks	"	" "
Robert Bicknell	"	" "
Geo. Bogard	"	" "
Charlotte Wallace	"	" "
John Hardesty	"	" "
Richard Brower	"	" "

HISTORY OF MARIA CREEK CHURCH. 113

Sarilda Donham	March	5, 1876
Calvin Thompson	Date not Recorded.	
Sarah Dunham	February	—, 1877
A. Casteel	March	18, "
Oliver Casteel	"	" "
Emily Wells	April	14, "
Sarah McArthur	January	19, 1878
James M. McArthur	"	" "
Lydia Elliott	"	" "
May Couchman	Date not Recorded,	
Louisa Warner	"	" "
Rosa Martin	"	" "
Nancy A. Couchman	"	" "
Clarinda Brower	"	" "
Wm. S. Bicknell	"	" "
J. W. Hammack	April	19, 1879
Clara Hammack	"	" "
Josie Hammack	"	" "
Ruth Wolf	November	9, 1879
Idelle Bicknell	"	" "
Ellen Morford	"	" "
Sarah E. Chambers	"	" "
Edna Wisner	"	" "
Alvira Walker	"	" "
Amanda Wolf	"	" "
Leoto Donham	"	" "
Edward Chambers	"	" "
Edward Townsly	"	" "
Edward Miller	"	" "
James Parker	"	" "
James Mewmaw	"	" "
James Townsly	"	" "
James Elliott	"	" "
James McCormack	"	" "

William Jarrell	November	9, 1879
William Donham	"	" "
Willis Regeway	"	" "
Newton Black	"	" "
Clarence Bicknell	"	" "
Spurgeon Keith	"	" "
Ellis Hooper	"	" "
Mary McCord	Date Not Recorded.	
M. A. Ferguson	"	" "
S. E. Ferguson	"	" "
Norman Guthrie	"	" "
Reta Ann Guthrie	"	" "
Henry F. Piper	"	" "
B. J. Robertson	"	" "
Ernest Bicknell		"
L. C. Bowen	January	17, 1880
Eli Logan	Date Not Recorded.	
Mary A. Logan	"	" "
A. Donham	February	14, 1880
John Hart	Date Not Recorded.	
Mrs. John Hart	"	" "
Jennie McArthur		1880
Ella Keith	January	18, 1881
Eva Walker	"	" "
Thomas Alsop		"
Lizzie Hagar	April	16, 1882
A. J. Lind	Date Not Recorded.	
Elizabeth Lind	"	" "
John G. Kimberlin	"	" "
Herman Piper	"	" "
Dollie Wells	October	1882
Delia Walker	November 19,	"
Josie Brackemeier	December 16,	"
William H. Jewell	Date Not Recorded.	

HISTORY OF MARIA CREEK CHURCH. 115

Martha Ward	May	6,	1883
Sophia Winkler	June	3,	"
Jennie Chanselor	"	17,	"
David S. Brooks	"	"	"
Edith Collins	August	24,	"
Eliza McKinley	November	4,	"
Orra Elliott	March	2,	1884
Hays Hedges	"	"	"
William Langford	"	"	"
Jennie Wells	April		"
Milton Hollingsworth	Date Not Recorded.		
Margaret A. Hollingsworth	"	"	"
Hannah J. Chambers	September		1884
Annie Robbins	May	3,	1885
Maggie West	November	25,	"
Sally Miller	"	"	"
Joseph Miller	"	"	"
Florence Robbins	"	"	"
Nancy E. West	"	"	"
Leota McNiece	No Date.		
Nancy Walker	December	19,	"
Samuel Miller	March	20,	1886
John Miller	"	"	"
Wilhelmina Miller	"	"	"
Augusta Cardochus	"	"	"
Flora Medley	July	4,	"
Anna Walker	"	"	"
Annie West	"	17,	"
John Pearce	September	19,	"
Charles Cardochus	October	17,	"
Ellen Pearce	November		1886
Jefferson Norton	"		"
Edward Lind	"		"
Lillie Wells	"		"

Mollie Hollingsworth	November	1886
Josephine Gibbs	,,	,,
Mattle Elliott	,,	,,
Anna Wells	,,	,,
Flora Richardson	,,	,,
Elizabeth Walker	,,	,,
Laura Mosier	December 19,	,,
Henry Vigus	February 13,	1887
Wallace Walker	May 29,	,,
Henry Miller	January	1888
Maggie Smith	,,	,,
Nancy Pinner	,,	,,
Harrison Wells	,,	,,
Mary Wells	,,	,,
William W. Richardson	March 18,	,,
William R. Strader	April 1,	,,
James Pinner	,, ,,	,,
Nellie Elliott	June 13,	,,
Emily Wells	Date not Recorded.	
Minnie Jones	,, ,,	,,
James Dellinger	,, ,,	,,
Cynthia Donham	,, ,,	,,
Nancy J. Hollingsworth	,, ,,	,,
Mary A. Hollingsworth	,, ,,	,,
Elizabeth J. Hollingsworth	,, ,,	,,
Mary Moore	August —,	1860
Harriet Irwin	,, ,,	,,
Rebecca J. Osborn	,, ,,	,,
Malissa Hooper	March ,,	1863
M. A. Ferguson	,, ,,	,,
S. E. Furgeson	,, ,,	,,
Frances Maxwell	,, ,,	,,
Lottie A. Bicknell	,, ,,	,,
Lacinda Moore	,, ,,	,,

STATISTICAL TABLE.

The following Statistical Table shows the number Baptized, Received by Letter and Relation; Restored, Dismissed by Letter, Excluded, and Deceased, and also the Total Membership in September of each year, as compiled from the Church Records, and from the Minutes of Union Association:

Year	Baptized.	Rec'd by Letter and Relation.	Restored.	Dismissed by Letter.	Excluded.	Deceased.	Total.	Year.	Baptized.	Rec'd by Letter and Relation.	Restored.	Dismissed by Letter.	Excluded.	Deceased.	Total.
1809	Charter Members,														13
1811		7					20	1837					1	1	84
1812	1	7		1			27	1838	26	3		1	2		110
1813							27	1839	3			7		5	93
1814	1	1					29	1840	4	1			1		96
1815		4					33	1841	5			19		1	81
1816	10	9	1	2	1		50	1842	1	2		2		2	80
1817	1	3		15			39	1843	*	*	*	*	*	*	*
1818	1	2		13	2		27	1844	1	4		1	4	3	105
1819	39	2		2	2		64	1845	1	8			3	1	109
1820	23	4		2	1		88	1846	4	3		11	2	4	99
1821	1	2		7	1		83	1847		2		1		4	96
1822		3		7			79	1848	2			2	1		95
1823		3		10	1		71	1849		4		1		1	96
1824	5	3	1		1	3	76	1850	8	12		1	2		112
1825	5	3	1	1			83	1851	16	2		23			106
1826	19	6		6			102	1852		2		2		5	101
1827		1		7	3	2	91	1853	25	7		2		4	130
1828	31	7		3	3		123	1854	4	5			4		135
1829	9	5		2			135	1855	12	9		4		2	152
1830	6	7		4	2		142	1856	21	3		14	2	2	160
1831	28	6		3	1	1	171	1857		3		4			159
1832	5	4		32	14	1	133	1858	7	4	1	20	7	3	141
1833			3	15	27		94	1859	1	7		3	2	3	141
1834			1	2	14	1	78	1860	25	1	3	4	1	3	162
1835	9	3		4	1	1	86	1861	1	1	2	7		1	158
1836	1	5	1	5	1	1	86	1862	17	1		6		3	167

STATISTICAL TABLE.—CONTINUED.

Year	Baptized.	Rec'd by Letter and Relation.	Restored.	Dismissed by Letter.	Excluded.	Deceased.	Total.	Year.	Baptized.	Rec'd by Letter and Relation.	Restored.	Dismissed by Letter.	Excluded.	Deceased.	Total.
1863	12	1		3	4	6	167	1876	17	1	1	5	2	2	138
1864	3	15			3	4	178	1877	8	1		3	1	3	140
1865	23	5		7	2	8	188	1878	1	4		9	6	3	192
1866	2	4		8	7	4	173	1879	4	4		4	4	2	108
1867	*	*	*	*	*	*	*	1880		1	2	2	3		113
1868		2		9	1	2	167	1881		7			1		119
1869		1		7	1		160	1882		5			2	2	120
1870	12	5		28	6	4	139	1883	6	3	1	17	5	3	105
1871		4		9		2	132	1884	7	2	1	6	0		109
1872	11	6	1	10	3	1	136	1885	1		2		1	2	109
1873		5		10	1	5	125	1886	7	6	1	1	3	2	118
1874		1		2	2	2	120	1887	16	1	1	6	4		126
1875	5	6		13		4	128	1888	5	4	1	12	1	1	122

ERRATA.

Page 94 Ephrai*n* West   should be   Ephria*m* West.
" 101 John Can*s*ellor   "   "   C*h*ancellor.
" 103 *Leander* Williams   "   "   *Leonard* Williams.
" 104 Eliza *C*albertson   "   "   Eliza Culbertson.
"   "   Gille*land* Arnold   "   "   Gille*ann* Arnold.
" 105 Eu*d*emile Chambers   "   "   En*d*emile Chambers.
" 111 Fred. Her*b*zog   "   "   Fred. Herzog.
" 112 Alpho*so* Chambers   "   "   Alpho*nso* Chambers.
" 113 James M*ew*maw   "   "   James M*u*maw.
" 114 Josie Brack*emeier*   "   "   Josie Brack*heimer*.
" 115 *Eliza* McKinley   "   "   *Celia* McKinley.
" 116 Matt*le* Elliott   "   "   Matt*ie* Elliott.

www.ingramcontent.com/pod-product-compliance
Lightning Source LLC
Chambersburg PA
CBHW020133170426
43199CB00010B/727